SHP
HISTORY
YEAR 7

THIS BOOK IS THE PROPERTY OF
THE KING'S SCHOOL
GIRLS' DIVISION MACCLESFIELD
and is lent to the pupil whose name is last
on the list below

Name	Form	Date Borrowed	Date Returned
Annabel Thomson	7WS	September 08	
Hannah Barker	7LAC		
Hope Sutton	7GoS		

No name may be crossed out or erased on this list.
Names may not be written elsewhere in this book.
Pupils are responsible for returning books when
finished with or when they leave. Books not
returned are charged at cost price.

SHP
HISTORY
YEAR 7

IAN DAWSON
MAGGIE WILSON

The Schools History Project

Set up in 1972 to bring new life to history for students aged 13–16, the Schools History Project continues to play an innovatory role in secondary history education. From the start, SHP aimed to show how good history has an important contribution to make to the education of a young person. It does this by creating courses and materials which both respect the importance of up-to-date, well-researched history and provide enjoyable learning experiences for students.

Since 1978 the Project has been based at Trinity and All Saints University College Leeds, from where it seeks to support, inspire and challenge teachers through INSET, the annual conference, a biennial Bulletin and the website: http://web.leedstrinity.ac.uk/shp. The Project is also closely involved with government bodies and exam boards in the planning of courses for Key Stage 3, GCSE and A level.

Although every effort has been made to ensure that website addresses are correct at time of going to press, Hodder Education cannot be held responsible for the content of any website mentioned in this book. It is sometimes possible to find a relocated web page by typing the address of the home page for a website in the URL window of your browser.

Hachette's policy is to use papers that are natural, renewable and recyclable products and made from wood grown in sustainable forests. The logging and manufacturing processes are expected to conform to the environmental regulations of the country of origin.

Orders: please contact Bookpoint Ltd, 130 Milton Park, Abingdon, Oxon OX14 4SB. Telephone: +44 (0)1235 827720. Fax: +44 (0)1235 400454. Lines are open 9.00–5.00, Monday to Saturday, with a 24-hour message answering service. Visit our website at www.hoddereducation.co.uk

First published in 2008
by Hodder Education,
part of Hachette Livre UK
338 Euston Road
London NW1 3BH

Impression number   10 9 8 7 6 5 4 3
Year   2012   2011   2010   2009   2008

Typeset in 12/14 pt Palatino Light
Layouts by Fiona Webb
Artwork by Art Construction, Jon Davis, Peter Bull, Steve Smith, Richard Duszczak and Tony Randell
Printed and bound in Italy

A catalogue record for this title is available from the British Library

ISBN 978 0 340 90733 7
Teacher's Resource Book ISBN 978 0 340 90734 4

Contents

Key features of SHP History

Before you start using this book here is a guide to help you get the most out it.

Enquiry This book is full of enquiry questions to investigate. Some short enquiries will only take one lesson. Other longer ones – the depth studies – may spread over a number of weeks.

Quick History These are overviews that sum up long periods in a short activity.

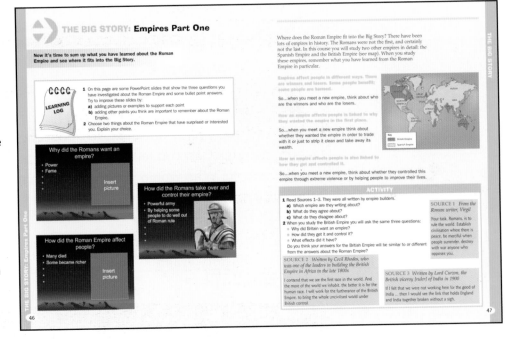

Banner introduces the enquiry and sums up what you are going to focus on.

Activities help you to build your enquiry step by step.

Big Story At the end of each section is a Big Story page that sums up the section and connects it to what is going to happen later. This is Part One and you will be doing Parts Two and Three later in the course, but they are all part of the same Big Story.

Themes Each section focuses on one thematic story. You will revisit each theme in later books. This section focuses on Empire.

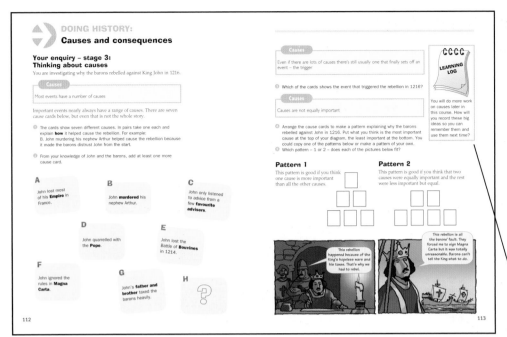

112
113

Doing History Each time you meet a new concept or process we recap the key ideas like this. If you want to get better at history this is what you focus on.

Learning Log helps you to record what you have learned so you can use it next time.

How to... Step-by-step explanations of important history skills or writing skills that will help you to improve your work.

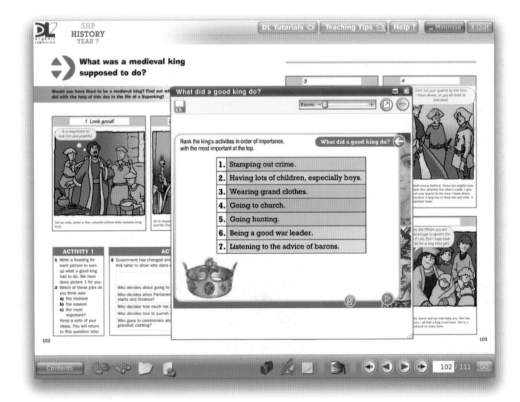

Dynamic Learning For every activity you will find on-screen activities and ICT-based investigations to help you

The mystery of the skeletons

These skeletons were found by archaeologists at Maiden Castle in the south of England. Use evidence to work out the story of these skeletons.

Amazing find at Maiden Castle: 52 skeletons dug up

STAGE 1 ▶

Ask questions

1. Look at the photo. Make a list of the questions you want to ask about these skeletons.

2 Study Clues A–D. Do they help to answer any of your questions?

CLUE A ▲ *Maiden Castle was a hillfort. It looked like this. The slopes were part of its strong defences. People lived here continuously for 500 years. Then around AD50 they deserted it.*

CLUE B ▼ *A Roman historian writing about the Britons (10BC–20AD)*

The Britons are war-mad, courageous and love fighting battles. They fight battles even if they have nothing on their side but their own strength and courage.

CLUE C ▲ *A close up of one of the skulls.*

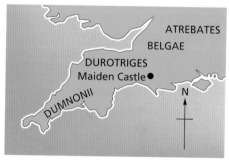

CLUE D ▲ *The British people were divided into tribes. This map shows the tribes that lived in southern England. The Durotriges tribe ruled the region around Maiden Castle.*

STAGE 3 ▶ Work out a hypothesis

A hypothesis is a possible explanation.

3 Read Professor Knowall's explanation of the story of the skeletons (right).
   a) Do Clues A–D **support** his ideas in any way?
   b) Do they **prove** he is right?

4 Write your own hypothesis about who you think these people were and what happened to them.

I know what happened. These skeletons were the people from the hillfort. They were killed in a savage attack by the neighbouring tribe – the Belgae. My evidence is the sword wound on the skull. The attackers slaughtered all the villagers and then just buried them as quickly as possible. I'm so clever!

In this table are the questions that Professor Knowall asked, and his answers. We think he has got some things right and some things wrong.

1 Question	2 Knowall's answer	3 Clues that tell you about this question	4 Your hypothesis	5 Are you completely or partly certain?
a) Who were the skeletons?	The Durotriges from Maiden Castle			
b) How did they die?	In a savage attack			
c) Who killed them?	The Belgae			
d) How were they buried?	Very quickly and carelessly			

Use Clues E–L to check his answers. Take each clue in turn.

1. Decide which question it helps you to answer. Reject any clues that don't help you at all! Note down the clue letter in column 3 on your own copy of the table.
2. Once you have looked at all the clues, write your own hypothesis in column 4.
3. In column 5, say how sure you are.
4. Once you have filled in your tables, discuss what you think Professor Knowall has got right and what you think he has got wrong.

CLUE **E** *Another of the skeletons found at Maiden Castle. Can you see what killed him?*

CLUE **F**

The only written evidence about what happened around Maiden Castle is this, written by a Roman historian called Suetonius. He says Vespasian, the commander of the Second Legion, 'fought 30 battles, conquered two warlike tribes and captured more than twenty large settlements'.

CLUE **G** The Roman army used a weapon like this called a ballista, a kind of catapult that could shoot an iron-headed bolt 300 metres.

CLUE **I**

The archaeologists at Maiden Castle uncovered 52 skeletons. There may be more still buried, but only part of the hillfort has been excavated.

- Fourteen of the 52 skeletons had wounds made by weapons.
- Most of these wounds were sword cuts on the skull.
- One skull had a hole made by a spear.

CLUE **J**

Four of the people lived on for some time after they were injured. We know this because the damaged bones had re-grown after the injury. Although we cannot tell exactly how long they lived for after their injuries we know it must have been many weeks or months. That is how long bone takes to start to heal.

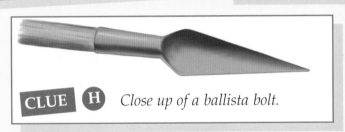

CLUE **H** Close up of a ballista bolt.

CLUE **L**

All the skeletons found at Maiden Castle were buried with objects to take to their next life. These objects included legs of meat and tankards of ale, pots, weapons, beads, rings and brooches.

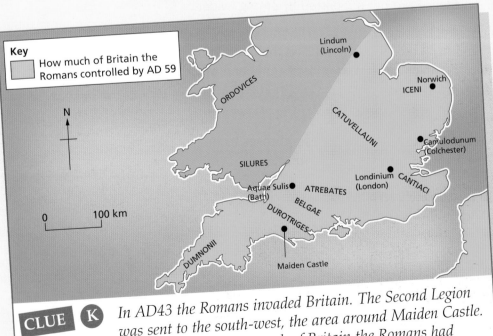

Key
How much of Britain the Romans controlled by AD 59

N

ORDOVICES

Lindum
(Lincoln)

Norwich
ICENI

CATUVELLAUNI

Camulodunum
(Colchester)

SILURES

Londinium
(London) CANTIACI

Aquae Sulis ATREBATES
(Bath)

BELGAE

DUROTRIGES

0   100 km

DUMNONII

Maiden Castle

CLUE **K** In AD43 the Romans invaded Britain. The Second Legion was sent to the south-west, the area around Maiden Castle. This map shows how much of Britain the Romans had conquered in 16 years.

It is almost time to write your final explanation. But first of all, learn an important lesson from the mistakes of Professor Knowall.

I know what happened. These skeletons were the people from the hillfort. They were killed in a savage attack by the neighbouring tribe – the Belgae. My evidence is the sword wound on the skull. The attackers slaughtered all the villagers and then just buried them as quickly as possible. So clever!

In History you have to back up your conclusions with evidence. The evidence is like a bridge that has to be strong enough to support your conclusion. If you have a flimsy evidence bridge you should not drive a big, certain conclusion across it. The evidence will not support it and the bridge will collapse! So in your explanation **remember not to pretend you are more certain than you are**. That was one of Professor Knowall's mistakes.

1. Which parts of Knowall's evidence are not supported by strong evidence?

2. Finally: Write your own paragraph giving your answer to the Mystery of the Skeletons. Include: who you think they were; who killed them; and how they were buried. Also include which clues were most helpful and why, and **how certain you are**.

... show how certain you are

You could choose from these phrases to help you express **how certain you are**.

It is completely certain that…
They probably…
They possibly…
I am very unsure…
We cannot be completely sure but…
My hypothesis is…
It is likely that…
They might have…

DOING HISTORY: What is History?

History isn't just about answering a teacher's questions. The best pupils at History are those who ask their own interesting and different questions and who think for themselves.

1. Which of your questions on page 2 were the best questions and why?

2. Work in groups. How many questions can you think of to ask about this picture in Source 1? Save your questions as you will find out more about it soon.

▼ SOURCE 1

In the Mystery of the Skeletons you used lots of clues. The proper word is 'source'. Sources give us evidence to help us answer our questions. Without sources we can't find out anything! There is a lot more about sources on pages 8–9.

Sometimes we can explain exactly what happened and why it happened. However, sometimes we can't be completely certain. This may be because:

- the sources may not give us all the information we want
- the sources may disagree and suggest different explanations.

3. Give one example of something you were not completely certain about in the Mystery of the Skeletons.

DOING HISTORY: Sources

Sources are so important in history that they get a special Doing History of their own.

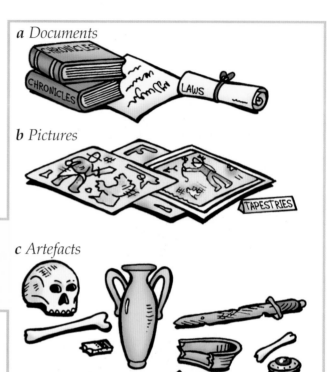

a Documents

b Pictures

c Artefacts

ACTIVITY

Work with a partner.
1 a) Work out which of sources 1–5 are documents (written sources) and which are artefacts (objects). That is not as easy as it sounds.
   b) Look back to pages 3–7. Find one other kind of artefact that is different from anything on this spread.
2 Which of sources 1–5 do you find most interesting – and why?
3 Choose one source on this spread. Write two things it tells you about the people who made it or what their life was like.
4 Choose one period of history that you studied at Key Stage 2. List three sources that give evidence about that period.
5 Name two sources that will tell future historians about life today but that did not exist 2000 years ago, at the time of the Romans.

▶ **SOURCE 1** *This pot full of silver coins was found in 1982 in Cambridgeshire. The coins were made by the Iceni people of East Anglia. The coins come from around AD50–60 and were probably hidden in the pot, then buried during a rebellion against the Romans.*

You saw this picture on page 7.
1 What questions did you ask about it?
2 Read the information in the caption below. Which of your questions can you now answer?

▼ **SOURCE 2** *A writing tablet found at a Roman fort on Hadrian's Wall in the north of England. It is made of wood. It is a letter to the wife of the commander of the Roman fort inviting her to a birthday party!*

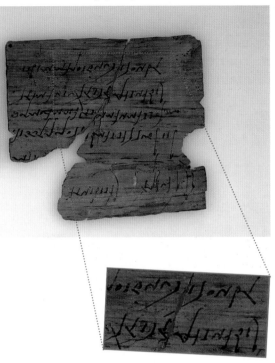

▼ **SOURCE 4** *This pot of Roman face cream was found in London in 2003. You can see the finger-marks made by the Roman lady who used it 2000 years ago.*

▼ **SOURCE 3** *An expensive Roman pottery bowl found in a ditch near Hadrian's Wall in the north of England. It had been sent all the way from France but had broken so someone had thrown it away.*

▼ **SOURCE 5** *This is the crest from a Roman centurion's helmet. It is made of horse hair. It was found next to a toy wooden sword. It was wet but otherwise had survived surprisingly well for 2000 years!*

A quick history of Britain before 1066

Sometimes you do history in depth – digging down into the detail. Sometimes you do history in overview. This is an overview. On the next eight pages there are 1000 years of British history and three groups of invaders – the Romans, Saxons and Normans. Your task is to decide who made the biggest difference to life in Britain. And remember – this is quick history!

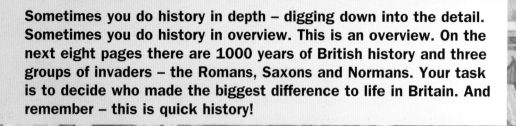

All the men learned to fight.

These are called round houses. The roofs and walls were very good at keeping the wind out.

They had to be on guard from attack from neighbouring tribes.

They collected their water from a well and their firewood from a nearby woodland.

10

Iron Age Britain: Maiden Castle AD40

This is what an English hillfort probably looked like 2000 years ago before the Romans came. This is Maiden Castle, which you examined in the Mystery of the Skeletons. Not everyone in England lived in a place like this but the lucky ones did.

These huts were for storing corn for the winter. They had enough food for the winter thanks to their good farmland.

ACTIVITY

Study the picture and the labels.
1 What kinds of work are people doing?
2 Choose some interesting words to describe their houses.
3 What can you find out about their religious beliefs?
4 Did their king rule all of Britain or just the local area?
5 Did they speak the same language that we do today?
6 If you were an invader why might you want to take over this place? Think of three reasons.
7 This period of history was called the Iron Age because people made things from iron. What can you find that is made of iron?

They all belonged to a tribe called the Durotriges. They were ruled by a king. One of the king's jobs was to defend the tribe from attack so he had to be a good fighter.

Growing food was their main activity. Everyone helped, including children. They had other fields outside the fort.

The totem pole was to fend off bad spirits. They worshipped the sun, the moon and other gods who they believed made sure of good harvests.

They made their own clothes and tools. But they got jewels and pottery from other countries.

They spoke their own local language. We don't know what it sounded like. No one ever recorded it or wrote it down!

Roman Britain: Canterbury AD250

This picture shows you an artist's impression of what Canterbury looked like in AD250 when the Romans had ruled Britain for 200 years.

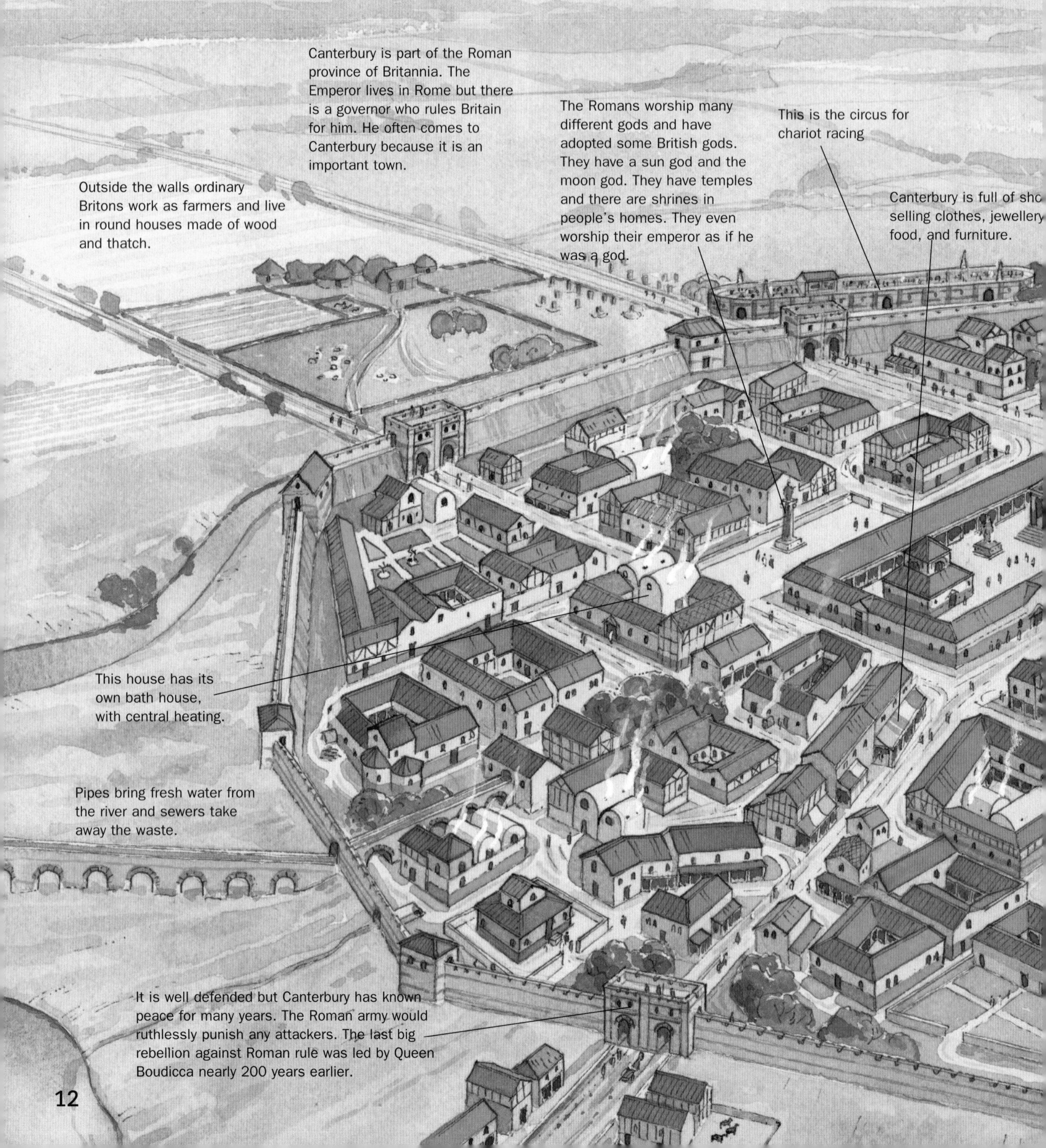

Canterbury is part of the Roman province of Britannia. The Emperor lives in Rome but there is a governor who rules Britain for him. He often comes to Canterbury because it is an important town.

The Romans worship many different gods and have adopted some British gods. They have a sun god and the moon god. They have temples and there are shrines in people's homes. They even worship their emperor as if he was a god.

This is the circus for chariot racing

Outside the walls ordinary Britons work as farmers and live in round houses made of wood and thatch.

Canterbury is full of sho selling clothes, jewellery food, and furniture.

This house has its own bath house, with central heating.

Pipes bring fresh water from the river and sewers take away the waste.

It is well defended but Canterbury has known peace for many years. The Roman army would ruthlessly punish any attackers. The last big rebellion against Roman rule was led by Queen Boudicca nearly 200 years earlier.

12

1 Compare the lives of the people in Roman Canterbury with the people at Maiden Castle on pages 10–11. Think about:
- the work people did
- the homes they lived in
- their religions
- who ruled them
- the languages they spoke.

a) Find as many differences as you can.

b) Find at least three similarities.

2 How much change did the Romans make? Give a mark out of 10 with 10 being 'huge change' and 0 being 'no change'.

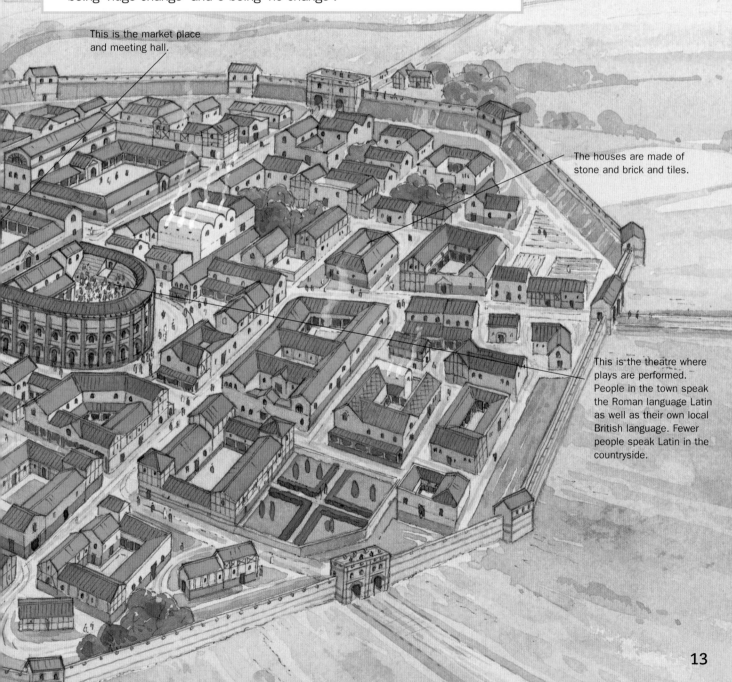

This is the market place and meeting hall.

The houses are made of stone and brick and tiles.

This is the theatre where plays are performed. People in the town speak the Roman language Latin as well as their own local British language. Fewer people speak Latin in the countryside.

Saxon England: Yorkshire in AD650

We have now moved forward 400 years. A lot has changed.

The Roman army left a long time ago. In around AD410 the city of Rome was under attack from invaders and the Emperor of Rome called his generals and their troops home to defend it.

That doesn't mean Britain was suddenly empty of people. The ordinary people stayed and carried on their lives as farmers and traders. But Britain was no longer defended by the Roman army so new invaders began to arrive because Britain was a rich country.

First the Angles and Saxons sailed over from north-western Europe (what we now call Germany). They settled all over England. They were an aggressive people. Britain split into lots of different kingdoms at war with each other. Two hundred years after the Romans had gone most people lived in villages like this one, West Heslerton in Yorkshire.

Changes in Anglo-Saxon England

- The Roman towns like Canterbury fell into decay. Sometimes they were ransacked by attackers but other times it was just that the skills and money needed to keep the towns going had gone.
- England (Angle-land) was used for the country for the first time.
- A new language appeared – English. Many common English words today come from the language brought by the Anglo-Saxons.
- Missionaries arrived from Europe and converted many people to Christianity. England became a Christian country. Everyone worshipped the one Christian God instead of many gods.

King Alfred

Around AD800 new invaders called Vikings came from Scandinavia. They stole from the monasteries, but later settled as traders.

Alfred, King of Wessex (in the south of England), pushed the Vikings back north. He became known as Alfred the Great. In the 900s England became one country again and has been ever since.

ACTIVITY

1 Was life in West Heslerton more like life in Maiden Castle (pages 10–11) or in Roman Canterbury (pages 12–13)? Look at the detail in the picture and read the text. Think about:
  - the work people did
  - the homes they lived in
  - their religions
  - who ruled them
  - the languages they spoke.
2 How much difference did the Saxons make? Give a mark out of 10 with 10 being 'huge changes' and 0 being 'no change'.

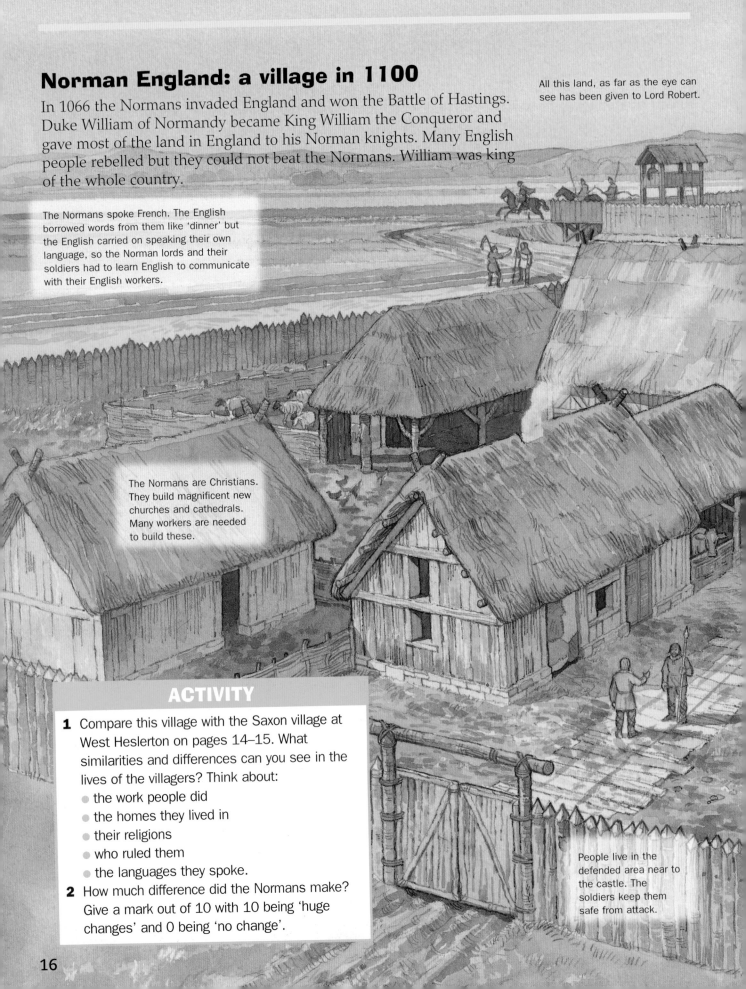

Norman England: a village in 1100

In 1066 the Normans invaded England and won the Battle of Hastings. Duke William of Normandy became King William the Conqueror and gave most of the land in England to his Norman knights. Many English people rebelled but they could not beat the Normans. William was king of the whole country.

All this land, as far as the eye can see has been given to Lord Robert.

The Normans spoke French. The English borrowed words from them like 'dinner' but the English carried on speaking their own language, so the Norman lords and their soldiers had to learn English to communicate with their English workers.

The Normans are Christians. They build magnificent new churches and cathedrals. Many workers are needed to build these.

People live in the defended area near to the castle. The soldiers keep them safe from attack.

ACTIVITY

1 Compare this village with the Saxon village at West Heslerton on pages 14–15. What similarities and differences can you see in the lives of the villagers? Think about:
  ● the work people did
  ● the homes they lived in
  ● their religions
  ● who ruled them
  ● the languages they spoke.
2 How much difference did the Normans make? Give a mark out of 10 with 10 being 'huge changes' and 0 being 'no change'.

16

The lord has built a castle here to control his land. The people have to work on his land. Lord Robert sets the rules now. His soldiers make sure he is obeyed.

Farming carries on much the same as ever. If people do not farm they do not eat.

People still collect water from the well; they still make their own clothes; they still eat the same food – soup and bread – and drink the same drink – ale.

SUMMARY ACTIVITY

Look back across your change scores on the last eight pages. Which invader (Roman, Saxons, Normans) made the biggest difference? Write a paragraph to explain your choice and be sure to back up your choice with some good reasons.

One aim of the quick history was to help you develop your sense of chronology. This means your overview of the past, your sense of when things happened and how history fits together.

A sense of chronology includes...

...putting people and events in the correct sequence in time.

1 Look back to the Mystery of the Skeletons (page 2). Did this event take place before or after the view of Maiden Castle shown on pages 10–11?
2 Put these people in the correct order: Saxons, Normans, Romans.

A sense of chronology includes...

...using the correct names for periods of history.

We divide the past into chunks that we call 'periods of history'. They are usually named after people or events. Periods are a useful way of dividing up the past.

3 Match each person A–G opposite with one of the periods. You could ask for some clues but it is better to think about what you know already to work it out.
4 Put the periods in order.
5 Where would you put each period on the timeline below?

A sense of chronology includes...

...being able to spot anachronisms.

An anachronism is something that is in the wrong period of history. Some anachronisms are obvious – for example if you imagined the Romans in Canterbury using a computer that would be an obvious anachronism. Others are harder to spot. See page 27 for examples.

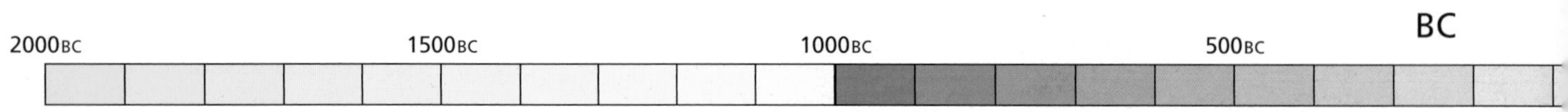

BC

| 2000BC | 1500BC | 1000BC | 500BC |

A

B

Tudors

C

D

Victorians

The Middle Ages

E

Ancient Egyptians

Romans

F

G

Ancient Greeks

Anglo-Saxons

AD

| AD500 | AD1000 | AD1500 | AD2000 |

19

THE BIG STORY:
Movement and Settlement Part One

Hello. My name's Ian Dawson and I've written most of the words, chosen the pictures and set the questions in this book. I want to introduce this page myself because it starts with my own family. I have set you two puzzles.

Puzzle 1

Uncle Frank

This is my Uncle Frank (on the left of the picture). I only met him once because he lived in Australia. In 1919, well before I was born, he sailed to Australia with hundreds of other British young men aged 16–19. They were recruited as workers by the Australian government to replace the many thousands of Australian men who had been killed in the First World War (1914–1918). When he was out there Frank married an Australian girl and lived the rest of his life in Australia.

❶ Look at the two people below. What do you think my Uncle Frank has in common with Barates and Mary Seacole?

Barates – a Roman soldier

This is the gravestone of Barates, a Roman soldier. It tells us that he was born in Palmyra (the country we now call Syria). He joined the Roman army and was sent to Britain. He spent the rest of his life there. He married a British girl. She changed her name to Regina, a popular Roman girl's name. When she died, Barates made her a beautiful carved tombstone. You can see both their tombstones in a museum in Newcastle.

Mary Seacole – a Jamaican nurse

Mary Seacole was born in Jamaica in 1805. She became famous as a healer and helped British soldiers who were based in Jamaica. When a war began between Britain and Russia she left Jamaica and travelled thousands of miles to the Crimea to help the British soldiers. Later she lived in London where she died in 1881.

Puzzle 2

Last year I investigated my family tree. I went back in time over 150 years, and discovered who my great-great-grandparents were. I found some real surprises. I am not going to tell you much else or that would spoil the puzzle. What do you think I found I had in common with the rest of the people on this page?

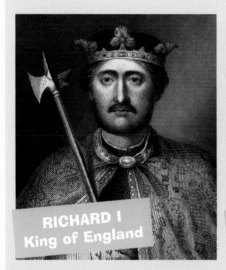

RICHARD I
King of England

MONTY PANESAR
England cricketer

JOHN REVIS
Retired surveyor

Richard I, King of England, was known as the Lionheart because he was a great soldier. He was born in Oxford. His great-grandfather was William the Conqueror (see pages 72–81 if you want to know more about William).

Monty Panesar, England cricketer, famous for his tricky spin bowling. He is a Sikh, which is why he always wears a patka (a smaller version of the full Sikh turban). His father came from the Punjab region of India in the 1970s to live in Luton.

John Revis, retired surveyor, born in Yorkshire but now living in Leicester. His father was a baker in Yorkshire.

MS DYNAMITE
Hip hop singer

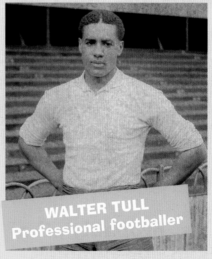

WALTER TULL
Professional footballer

Ms Dynamite (real name Niomi McLean-Daley) is a singer of hip hop music. She grew up in North London. Her mother, a primary school teacher, was Scottish and her father was Jamaican. It has been stated that she also has English, Irish, German, Grenadian and Barbadian ancestry.

Walter Tull, one of the first black professional footballers (Tottenham Hotspur and Northampton Town) and the first black officer in the British army. He was killed in action in 1918 during the First World War. Walter's father was born in Barbados, came to England and married a girl from Kent.

THE BIG STORY:

Movement and Settlement Part One continued

How did you get on with the puzzles?

You probably worked out for Puzzle 1 that Uncle Frank, Barates and Mary Seacole all left the country they were born in and migrated (moved) somewhere else.

What about Puzzle 2? When I investigated my family tree I discovered that one of my great-great-grandfathers was born in Copenhagen in Denmark in 1806 and he came to Liverpool as an engineer. Another came from Ireland in the 1850s and worked with horses as a groom and ostler. If I investigated further back in time I'd probably find more migrants. So that is what we six have in common: we're all related to immigrants.

The person who was most surprised about this was John Revis. He had traced his family back to the 1700s and they were all born in Britain so he didn't think he had links to any other country. A branch of his family had moved to America but it seemed no one had moved to Britain from anywhere else. Then scientists investigating the movement of people round the world asked him if they could investigate his DNA. They discovered that he was descended from an African who came to Britain probably with the Romans. There is evidence that Africans came to Britain as Roman slaves and as soldiers in the Roman army. His ancestors could have been either.

I want you to remember two important things from my family puzzles:

A People have always moved and settled in other places and other lands

Sometimes they move between countries. Sometimes they move within a country.

Sometimes they move because they want to; sometimes they are forced. Sometimes they come as invaders to take over a country. Sometimes they come as peaceful settlers. But all through history people move and settle.

🔵 Look back to pages 10–17.
   a) Which four groups of people came to Britain and settled here?
   b) Why did they move?

B Most of us, probably all of us, have migrants in our families

I found out that migration was part of my story. Migration is probably also part of your story.

🔵 Think about Uncle Frank, Barates and Mary Seacole on page 20. Would you call them immigrants (people who come to a country) or emigrants (people who leave a country)? Think carefully – it's a trick question!

How are you going to record what you have learned?

In Key Stage 3 History you are going to follow a number of Big Stories through time. The Quick History and the puzzles on the previous pages are Part One of this Big Story of Movement and Settlement. When you come back to this story you'll need to remember what you have learned. There are many ways to do this. Here is one idea.

I've used a map to record examples of Movement and Settlement. It's such a simple map that I haven't tried to draw Britain accurately. There's no need because the important information is in the labels. I've also added some small drawings to remind me why people moved and settled in other places.

③ What else from pages 10–25 could you add to this diagram?

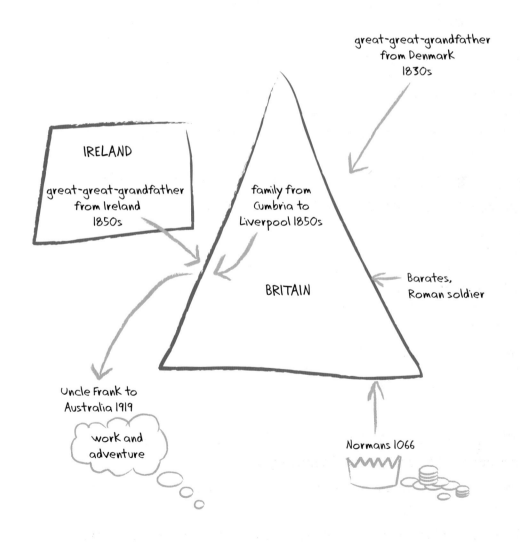

great-great-grandfather
from Denmark
1830s

IRELAND

great-great-grandfather
from Ireland
1850s

family from
Cumbria to
Liverpool 1850s

Barates,
Roman soldier

BRITAIN

Uncle Frank to
Australia 1919

work and
adventure

Normans 1066

DOING HISTORY: Big Stories

Doing History is a bit like a doing a jigsaw. Sometimes you spend time sorting out the detailed part of the puzzle as I did with my own family history. But your aim is to eventually connect it to the big picture. That is what the Big Story pages in this book are all about. They help you connect the little stories that make history interesting into the big stories, across time, that help you understand the past.

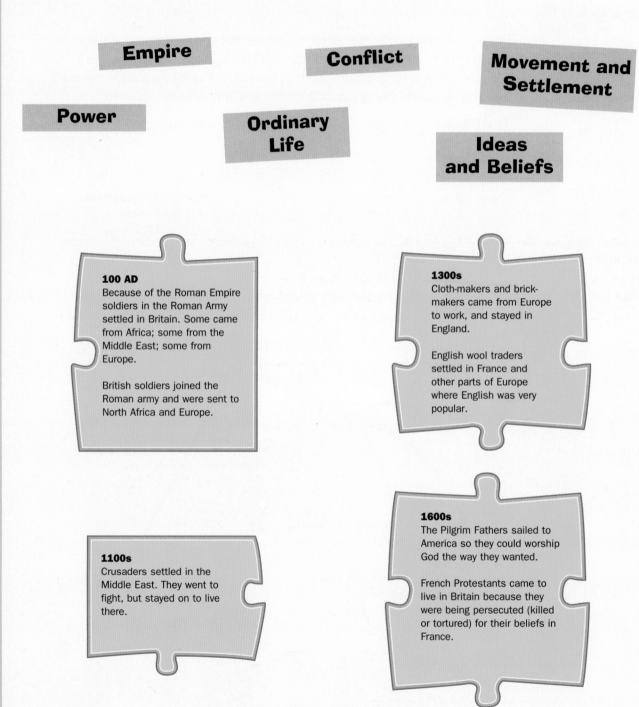

Empire

Conflict

Movement and Settlement

Power

Ordinary Life

Ideas and Beliefs

100 AD
Because of the Roman Empire soldiers in the Roman Army settled in Britain. Some came from Africa; some from the Middle East; some from Europe.

British soldiers joined the Roman army and were sent to North Africa and Europe.

1300s
Cloth-makers and brick-makers came from Europe to work, and stayed in England.

English wool traders settled in France and other parts of Europe where English was very popular.

1100s
Crusaders settled in the Middle East. They went to fight, but stayed on to live there.

1600s
The Pilgrim Fathers sailed to America so they could worship God the way they wanted.

French Protestants came to live in Britain because they were being persecuted (killed or tortured) for their beliefs in France.

ACTIVITY

Each jigsaw piece tells a little story that fits into the Big Story of Movement and Settlement.

1 Look back to pages 10–23.

   a) Find examples to fit with two of the pieces.

   b) Add two more pieces to add more detail to the story.

2 The Big Story has not ended. What would you write on a jigsaw piece for this decade to bring this story up to date?

The Big Stories help us

…to see links between people and events across time

The Big Stories help us

…to understand what's happening today

1. Use the Big Story on the jigsaw pieces on these two pages to give one example of each of the two Key Points above.

2. Why do you think we've made the Big Story pieces look like a jigsaw?

3. What should you be able to do and understand about the Big Stories when you have finished Key Stage 3 History that you can't do now?

1700s
People found guilty of crimes in England were transported to America and later to Australia.

Black people were brought to Britain as servants, or slaves.

1950s
Many people from the West Indies came to Britain after the Second World War because Britain needed a lot more workers in hospitals and schools, on trains and buses, in factories and building sites – to rebuild Britain after the war.

Britons migrated to Australia, Canada and other places to start a new life.

1850s
In Ireland a disease ruined the potato crop on which the Irish people depended. More than a million starved to death. More than a million others migrated to the USA and to England to look for work and food.

In Britain people left farming jobs in the countryside and moved to cities to find jobs in the factories.

Today

How to do well in Key Stage 3 History

1 Which of the speakers below do you think will do really well in History? Give reasons.

2 Which of them do you think might do less well? Give reasons.

3 Can you think of anything else that would help you to do well in History?

4 What do you think makes History:
  a) similar to other subjects?
  b) different from other subjects?

1 I'm good at learning and remembering dates.

2 I'm good at thinking of questions to ask.

3 I always write very neatly.

4 In my notebook I underline my headings in a different colour every week.

5 I don't believe everything I'm told. I like checking things out for myself.

6 I'm good at drawing pictures of battles and ships.

7 I am interested in why things happen.

8 I'm good at copying down exactly what the teacher tells us.

9 I like coming up with my own answers using all the evidence I can find.

10 I'm really interested in people.

11 I like making PowerPoint presentations.

12 I like visiting old castles and museums.

13 I like stories.

14 I am good at making connections.

26

ACTIVITY 2

You'll do even better in History if you use the right vocabulary!
Can you explain what these words mean?

Source　　　　　　　　**Archaeology**

Chronological order

Hypothesis　　　　**Anachronism**

Medieval　　　　**Document**

Artefact

ACTIVITY 3

If you drew a picture of a Roman town and included a train, the train would be an anachronism because it did not exist in Roman times.
An anachronism is something that is in the wrong period of time.

There are five anachronisms hidden in this picture of a Roman street.
How many can you find?

The Roman Empire

The quick history of Britain leads into another of our big stories – the story of Empire. Have you ever wondered why the Romans invaded Britain in the first place? It was because they wanted to build their empire. The same thing happened, 1000 years later. Empires are important in history. They change things! They affect people! They cause wars! And sometimes they bring peace!

So understanding empires is an important part of understanding history. Later on in this course you will study the British Empire, which was the biggest the world had ever known, and you will discover many similarities to the story of the Roman Empire.

We are going to use three questions to investigate the Roman Empire, and you will find that these are questions that you can ask about any empire:

- Why did they want it?
- How did they get it and control it?
- How did it affect people?

But first things first…

Where was the Empire?

The Roman Empire was enormous! (See map below.) It included many races from many different countries.

What is an empire?

Imagine your school is so powerful it takes over the other local schools. Your headteacher tells the schools what to do. They send you their best pupils who do all your homework. They also give you money so that you can buy extra computers plus comfy chairs, the best school meals and designer clothes. What a life! They do this because they are scared of you. You have an army that would force them to obey if they showed signs of resisting. In return, you loan them some of your best teachers and help them improve their buildings but you get far more out of the situation than they do. This would be your school's *empire*. An empire is when one supremely powerful country takes over other countries and rules them for its own benefit.

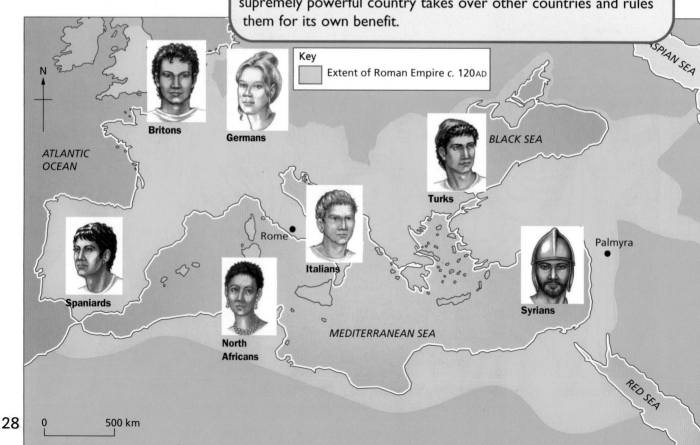

Key

☐ Extent of Roman Empire *c.* 120AD

N

ATLANTIC OCEAN

Britons

Germans

CASPIAN SEA

BLACK SEA

Turks

Rome

Italians

Palmyra

Spaniards

North Africans

Syrians

MEDITERRANEAN SEA

RED SEA

0   500 km

Into the mind of an empire builder!

Meet Paulinus. He was the Governor of Britain (the Romans called it Britannia) in AD60. He had helped conquer Britain and now he was its governor. If we could ask him why Rome wanted an empire, what might he say?

> Every country we conquer makes Rome wealthier. We collect taxes from everyone in the Empire. Britannia pays high taxes because it has silver mines.

> The Empire improves people's lives. When we take over a country we help them build towns and better houses with fresh water supplies. They can buy luxury goods like jewellery and pottery from every other part of the Empire.

> Rome is a huge city, full of people who need food. We order every part of the Empire to send food to Rome to keep the Romans happy. Britannia has lots of rich farming land so it sends lots of food.

> As a general, I know that the best way to become famous is to win new lands for the Empire. If a general conquers a new country he is given a victory march through Rome. The crowds will cheer, and he will become a wealthy man with lots of land and slaves.

> Rich Romans don't do hard work for themselves. They have slaves to do that for them. So Rome needs a constant supply of slaves. When there is a rebellion or a war we can take the prisoners and make them slaves and send them to build our fine buildings.

> Because we have a strong army we bring law and order to every part of our empire. People don't dare rebel.

ACTIVITY

1 Which of these reasons would Paulinus use to persuade:

   a) the Roman Emperor that Britannia should stay part of the Empire?

   b) British leaders that it was good to be part of the Roman Empire?

2 Which reason would be most important to Paulinus himself?

3 What would you ask or say to Paulinus if you were a Briton at the time?

Why was the Roman army like a top football team?

How could one city, Rome, control an empire that stretched over thousands of miles? The most important reason was the Roman army. Find out what made it so successful as you compare the Roman army to a top football team!

⚽ The best equipment

There were two types of soldier: legionaries and auxiliaries. The legionaries were armed with a javelin, sword, dagger and shield and protected by body armour. Weapons and armour were constantly improved as new ideas were tested. Some legions had larger weapons, such as the ballista (see page 5).

⚽ Total commitment

All soldiers were volunteers. They stayed in the army for 25 years and they were not allowed to marry. They were sent anywhere in the Empire, usually far away from their homeland. The army became their family. The best soldiers became centurions, in charge of 80 other men.

⚽ Good rewards

Roman soldiers were paid well. They got good food and every fort had a hospital and baths. They lived better than most civilians. After 25 years the legionaries retired and were given a pension of about ten years' pay or a small farm.

⚽ Mobility

The Romans built straight roads so their soldiers and cavalry could get from fort to fort very quickly.

Legionary: heavily armed footsoldiers

Auxiliary: lightly armed, faster-moving troops, including some cavalry (horsemen)

⚽ Excellent training and fitness

Roman soldiers trained hard. They learned to use their weapons, fight together and follow orders precisely. They had to be able to march 32 km in five hours carrying their full kit which included: two swords; a spear and shield; a thick cloak for warmth and to sleep in; two posts for making a defensive camp at night; a cooking pot, bowl and spoon; a spade, pick or axe; food for three to four days; and a bag with spare boots, money, dice, etc.

⚽ International squad

To start with, most soldiers in the Roman army came from Italy. That soon changed. As the Romans conquered new territory they got the best local fighters to join the army. In the first 60 years after the Romans conquered Britain, at least 9000 British men joined the army and were sent abroad to fight for Rome. In AD120, when Hadrian's Wall was built, hardly any of the soldiers were from Italy. They came from all over the Empire: France, Spain, Hungary, Syria, Algeria and Iraq.

⚽ Discipline and tactics

The Romans used ruthless tactics to keep soldiers loyal. If there was a mutiny, they would 'decimate' the unit – killing every tenth soldier. They were equally ruthless in punishing rebellious people. They scared people into submission. Latest estimates suggest that out of a population of 2 million Britons about 100,000 were killed by Roman soldiers. They also used clever battle tactics, for example, the testudo (which means tortoise). (See the photo.)

1. Why was this formation called a testudo?
2. Why would it have been effective in battle?
3. What does it tell you about the skills and training of a Roman soldier?

ACTIVITY

1 Here are some tips for success in football management.

• *Buy the best players from around the world.*
• *Get them fit! Keep them healthy!*
• *Pay them well.*
• *Stay in the best hotels.*
• *Banish wives and girlfriends (WAGs).*
• *Clever tactics – use your brain.*
• *Get your players (and supporters) to the games on time!*

How are these similar to what made the Roman army successful?

2 Design a recruitment poster for the Roman army. You can include up to twenty words, telling people about the advantages of joining the army.

3 Which two features of the Roman army do you think were most important in helping Romans conquer and control their empire?

Did people love or hate living in the Roman Empire?

Now it's time to investigate how individual people felt about the Roman Empire. Did they love being part of the Empire? Did they hate it? Explore the lives of some fascinating and famous people and work out where they go on our love–hate line.

ACTIVITY 1

The line below shows whether people loved or hated living in the Roman Empire – or something in-between. Here are two people from places you have already visited.

Esca, who died at the hillfort at Maiden Castle

Drusilla, a lady who lived in Roman Canterbury

These pupils have placed them on the line.

1 Do you agree with where these pupils have placed the people? If not, move them.
2 Write a speech bubble for each character to explain their position on the line.

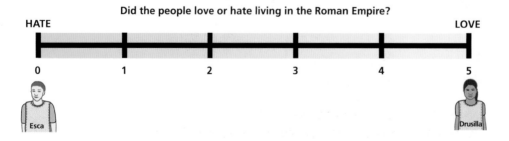

Did the people love or hate living in the Roman Empire?

HATE   LOVE

0   1   2   3   4   5

Esca   Drusilla

32

ACTIVITY 2

True or False?

And while you're exploring these people on pages 34–41 find out whether each of these statements is true or false!

1 One Roman Emperor began his working life as a teacher.

2 If you went to the games, you were more likely to see lions attacking sheep than lions fighting gladiators.

3 Some criminals were executed by being sewn into a bag with poisonous snakes and thrown into a river.

4 The Romans cleaned their clothes in urine.

3 Here are four more people to place on the line.

- Cogidumnus of the Atrebates people of southern Britain
- Barates, a soldier
- Rufrius, a merchant
- Boudicca, Queen of the Iceni people of East Anglia.

a) Read the bubbles and decide who is speaking: Cogidumnus, Barates, Rufrius or Boudicca.

b) Decide where to put them on the love–hate line.

> I was a powerful British leader but the Romans decided to take my land and make my people give up their weapons. We rebelled, destroyed the Roman cities and killed as many Romans as we could find.

> I came to Londinium from Spain to make my fortune. I did well and used my money to build a good new house for my family. Then Boudicca rebelled. We escaped from Londinium just in time but the rebels burned my home. Now I have nothing left.

> I was a powerful British leader but I realised that the Romans were too strong to fight. I helped them take over Britain. In return they built me a wonderful palace at Fishbourne and let me keep my lands and riches.

> I was born far away from Britannia, in Syria, where the sun shines every day. I joined the Roman army and served all over the Empire. In Britannia I married Regina, a British girl, but now, alas, she is dead. I retired from the army but still live in Britannia, far from my birthplace.

Now you are going to investigate four more people on pages 34–41.

4 Divide into groups. Each group should take one of these four people.

a) Decide where your person should go on the love–hate line.

b) Write a speech bubble to sum up your person's opinion of the Roman Empire.

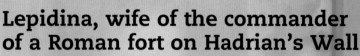

Lepidina, wife of the commander of a Roman fort on Hadrian's Wall

Vindolanda, Britannia, AD105

I am going to a party! Listen to what my dear friend Claudia writes in her letter.

> On September 11th, sister, for the day of my birthday, I send you a warm invitation to come to us, to make the day more enjoyable for me. Give my greetings to your husband, Cerealis.

A party! That will be a change from all the tiresome days in this boring fort. It's all my father's fault. He chose Cerealis as my husband. 'He's a good, steady man,' he said. What girl wants a good, steady man for her husband, especially when he's twenty years older than me and gets posted to such dull places? The army orders our husbands across the Empire and we women must follow wherever they go. My friend, Marcia, has followed her husband from Arabia to Mesopotamia to Germania and finally here to miserable, damp Britannia. Poor girl. I wonder where I will end up?

See instructions on page 33.

Roman men think that we women are not intelligent enough to run our own lives. Our fathers choose our husbands and, if my husband dies, the law says I have to go back to my father or my brother because a woman must have male guardians all her life.

It's different for women in Britannia. Here, women are more independent although, to be honest, independence looks hard work to me.

The legionaries are not allowed to marry until they have completed their 25 years, but many have British 'wives'. The families live in the village outside the fort.

The wives are always working, caring for children, spinning, weaving, cleaning, cooking, collecting water and they don't have any slaves to do it for them.

I'd like to buy Claudia a pretty pair of boots but the village shops are full of cheap things. They're good enough for the soldiers' families but not for the commander's wife. Will I ever go shopping in Rome or even Londinium again?

35

Diocles

Rome, AD140

Yes, it really is me, you're not mistaken. I am Diocles, the Great, the Magnificent, the most famous charioteer in the entire history of Rome! I know, I look even more handsome in real life than in all those pictures of me on vases and mosaics!

I am the greatest charioteer of them all. I have driven in over 4200 races and won 1400 of them. No one has ever come close to matching that! It all seems a long way from my days as a slave in Hispania. I was one of the lucky ones, I don't deny it. Thanks be to the gods that my skill with horses was spotted early on. I probably wouldn't be here otherwise.

See instructions on page 33.

Chariot racing is the best sport in Rome. Listen to the noise! Oh, that sounds like another charioteer has fallen. We really do put our lives on the line every night to entertain the crowds. It's paid off for me as I'm rich now, but many of my friends have fallen beneath the chariot's wheels. Hearing the charging horses and the roaring crowds still makes the hairs on the back of my neck stand up! It certainly beats watching those gladiators. My mate Scorpius the Gladiator says he's now so valuable that his owner protects him. It's too risky to put him in the arena with a lion so most of his contests are easy wins or fixed so the result is a draw. He says the arena's more like a zoo these days with lions chasing sheep and pigs rather than gladiators fighting each other!

One day I will retire, but with my money and good looks I should be fine for another few years.

And yes, of course I'll sign an autograph for you. My pleasure!

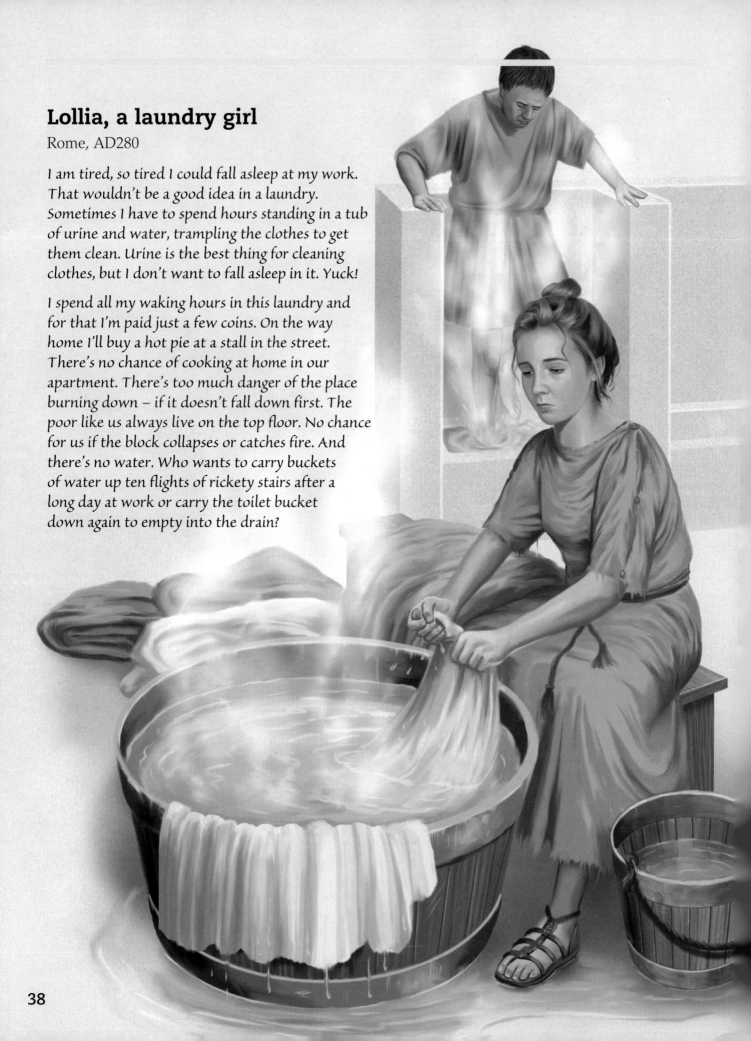

Lollia, a laundry girl

Rome, AD280

I am tired, so tired I could fall asleep at my work. That wouldn't be a good idea in a laundry. Sometimes I have to spend hours standing in a tub of urine and water, trampling the clothes to get them clean. Urine is the best thing for cleaning clothes, but I don't want to fall asleep in it. Yuck!

I spend all my waking hours in this laundry and for that I'm paid just a few coins. On the way home I'll buy a hot pie at a stall in the street. There's no chance of cooking at home in our apartment. There's too much danger of the place burning down – if it doesn't fall down first. The poor like us always live on the top floor. No chance for us if the block collapses or catches fire. And there's no water. Who wants to carry buckets of water up ten flights of rickety stairs after a long day at work or carry the toilet bucket down again to empty into the drain?

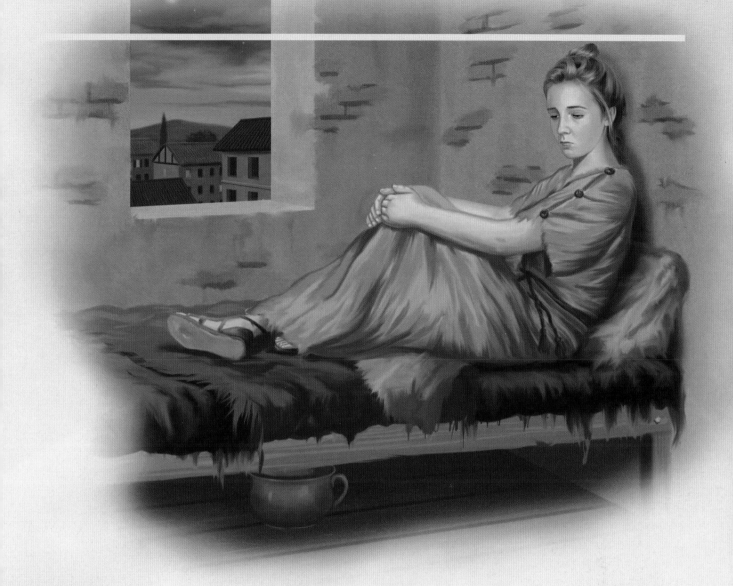

There are slaves who are better off than I am. One slave girl who brings her mistress's clothes to the laundry is being taught to read and write. I bet she even has her own nice little bed. Many slaves get rich when their masters give them their freedom. We all know the story of Pertinax, a slave's son. He started as a teacher, then joined the army, ended up a general – and then became Emperor. He was soon assassinated, mind you. Serves him right for getting above himself!

I'm free but I live in squalor. I'll be lucky if I live to be 30. Isn't freedom wonderful!

Still, it can't be all good being a slave. If one slave in the house tries to murder the master then they all get tortured and crucified, whether they were involved or not!

Most punishments are violent like that. If a man kills his father, then he's tied up in a sack with poisonous snakes and thrown into the river! Who thought that up?

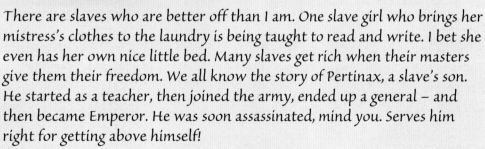

See instructions on page 33.

Horatius, a wealthy man

Lullingstone, Britannia, AD350

Come in, come in. Welcome to my humble home! You're the first to arrive so I'll give you a guided tour. Everyone else should be here later.

First I'll show you around the bath house. You're going to love it! We have hot, warm and cold pools. The hot pool is quite large so all of us should be able to use it together – we can catch up on business. It's so inconvenient going to the town baths and having to share the water with all those strangers. They do like to listen in to what you're saying – I suppose it adds a bit of excitement to their lives, but it's all very irritating! Anyway, I've asked the slaves to add the oils and perfumes to the pool, so it may be difficult to keep awake in there, but it should feel great! And don't let me forget to give you the face cream I've had sent from Londinium. It's supposed to be quite miraculous!

Please use the slaves as if they were your own. They're very well trained so if there's anything at all you need, please just ask them.

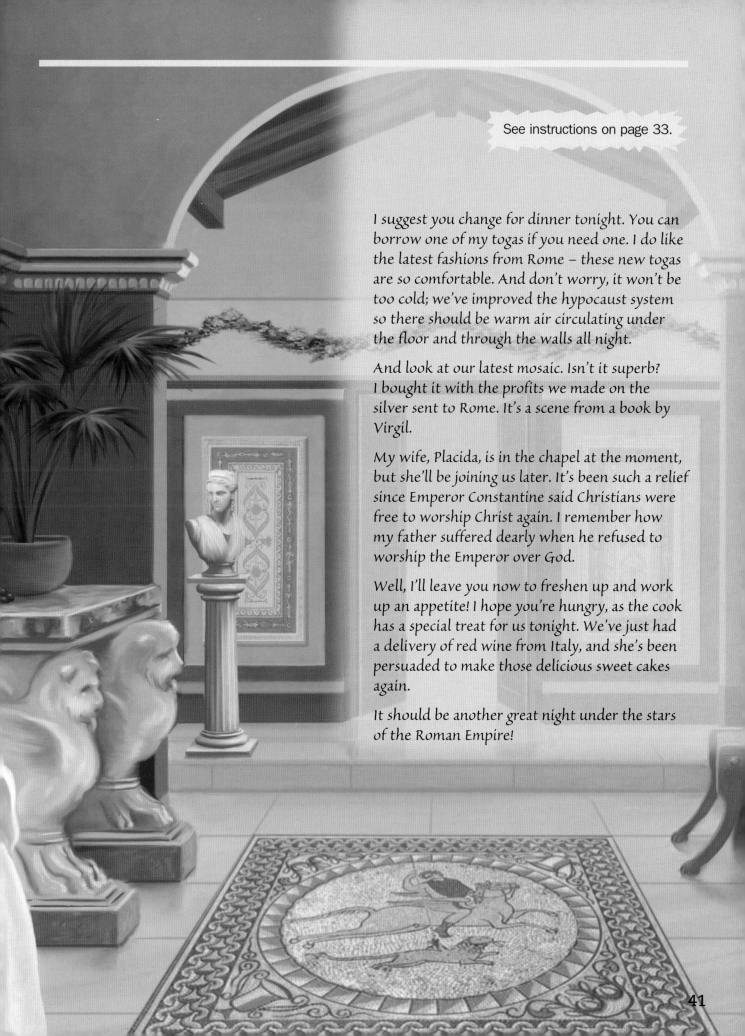

See instructions on page 33.

I suggest you change for dinner tonight. You can borrow one of my togas if you need one. I do like the latest fashions from Rome – these new togas are so comfortable. And don't worry, it won't be too cold; we've improved the hypocaust system so there should be warm air circulating under the floor and through the walls all night.

And look at our latest mosaic. Isn't it superb? I bought it with the profits we made on the silver sent to Rome. It's a scene from a book by Virgil.

My wife, Placida, is in the chapel at the moment, but she'll be joining us later. It's been such a relief since Emperor Constantine said Christians were free to worship Christ again. I remember how my father suffered dearly when he refused to worship the Emperor over God.

Well, I'll leave you now to freshen up and work up an appetite! I hope you're hungry, as the cook has a special treat for us tonight. We've just had a delivery of red wine from Italy, and she's been persuaded to make those delicious sweet cakes again.

It should be another great night under the stars of the Roman Empire!

As you have looked at the impact of the Roman Empire on different people you have probably built up a love–hate line something like this.

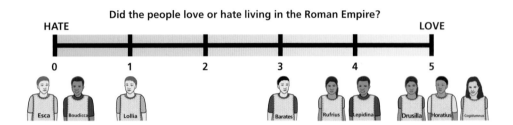

Did the people love or hate living in the Roman Empire?

HATE   LOVE

0   1   2   3   4   5

Esca Boudicca   Lollia   Barates   Rufrius Lepidina   Drusilla Horatius Cogidumnus

It is clear that some people did well out of the Roman Empire but others did badly. Others were somewhere in between. So here are two Key Points about Diversity that hopefully make sense now you've completed the investigation.

People's lives are different

… even if they live in the same period of history

People's lives are different

… even if they live in the same country in the same period of history

ACTIVITY 1

1 Use your completed love–hate line to choose examples to support each of the two key points above.

2 Discuss: If you did a love–hate line to show what people thought about living in Britain today would you expect similar or different results?

DOING HISTORY: Interpretations

Interpretations are different versions of the past. All kinds of people create interpretations of the past – film-makers and museum designers, people who write books or websites, people who take part in living history events.

And the tricky thing about these people is: they often give you different versions about the past. So here are our Key Points about Interpretations:

Different people

… tell different stories about the past

Different people

… tell different stories about the past by including some people, topics or evidence and leaving out or down-playing others

ACTIVITY 2

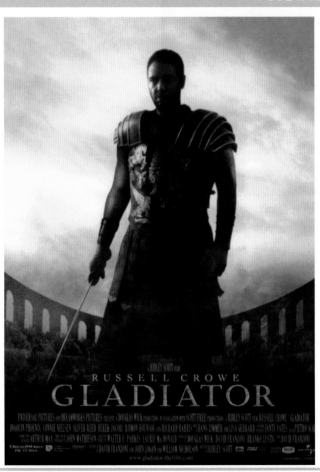

3 Look carefully at this film poster.
  a) Which of these words best fit this interpretation of the Roman Empire: cruel, rich, exotic, grand, heroic, mysterious, fun, dull?
  b) Which details in the poster make you think of these words?
4 Which aspects of life in the Roman Empire do you think this film:
  a) includes?
  b) leaves out?
5 How would interpretations of the Roman Empire be different in two books – one about Lollia and one about Horatius (see pages 38–41)?

LEARNING LOG

You will do more work on Diversity and Interpretations later in the course. How will you record these big ideas so you can remember them and use them next time? Don't just copy out what we've said.

If you visit Hadrian's Wall you might meet a Roman soldier. He won't be a ghost – he's an actor playing the part of a Roman. I met one of these Romans recently. He told me about all the things the Romans did to improve life in Britain. That's what started the argument. Why do you think I disagreed with him?

ACTIVITY

1 Which rocks can:
   a) the Roman re-enactor choose to support his interpretation?
   b) I choose to support my interpretation?
2 Do you think any of the rocks are so important that they should count as double?
3 a) Which interpretation do you agree with? The Roman Empire was:
   - a good thing
   - a bad thing.
   b) What are the main reasons for your choice?
4 People often disagree about whether empires are a good or a bad thing. Think of as many reasons as possible why there are different interpretations of empires.

44

Water supplies

Roman army

Entertainment

Building skills

Baths and heating

Taxes

Slavery

Ruled by Rome

Trade

Thousands killed in conquests

Deaths in rebellions

Travel

Now it's time to sum up what you have learned about the Roman Empire and see where it fits into the Big Story.

LEARNING LOG

1 On this page are some PowerPoint slides that show the three questions you have investigated about the Roman Empire and some bullet point answers. Try to improve these slides by:

a) adding pictures or examples to support each point

b) adding other points you think are important to remember about the Roman Empire.

2 Choose two things about the Roman Empire that have surprised or interested you. Explain your choice.

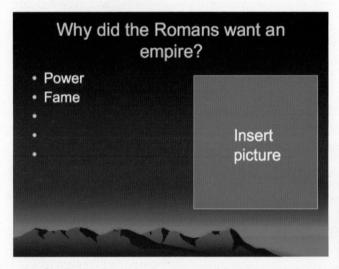

Why did the Romans want an empire?

- Power
- Fame
-
-
-

Insert picture

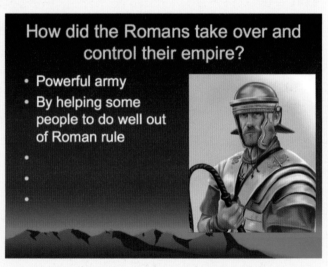

How did the Romans take over and control their empire?

- Powerful army
- By helping some people to do well out of Roman rule
-
-
-

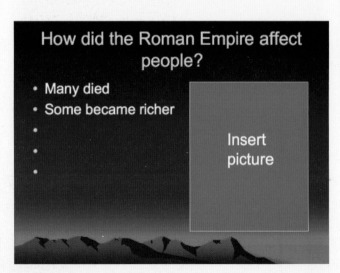

How did the Roman Empire affect people?

- Many died
- Some became richer
-
-
-

Insert picture

Where does the Roman Empire fit into the Big Story? There have been lots of empires in history. The Romans were not the first, and certainly not the last. In this course you will study two other empires in detail: the Spanish Empire and the British Empire (see map). When you study these empires, remember what you have learned from the Roman Empire in particular.

Empires affect people in different ways. There are winners and losers. Some people benefit; some people are harmed.

So…when you meet a new empire, think about who are the winners and who are the losers.

How an empire affects people is linked to why they wanted the empire in the first place.

So…when you meet a new empire think about whether they wanted the empire in order to trade with it or just to strip it clean and take away its wealth.

How an empire affects people is also linked to how they got and controlled it.

So…when you meet a new empire, think about whether they controlled this empire through extreme violence or by helping people to improve their lives.

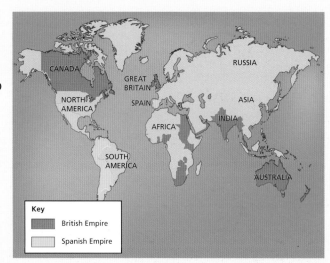

Key
◼ British Empire
◻ Spanish Empire

ACTIVITY

1 Read Sources 1–3. They were all written by empire builders.
   a) Which empire are they writing about?
   b) What do they agree about?
   c) What do they disagree about?
2 When you study the British Empire you will ask the same three questions:
   ● Why did Britain want an empire?
   ● How did they get it and control it?
   ● What effects did it have?
   Do you think your answers for the British Empire will be similar to or different from the answers about the Roman Empire?

SOURCE 1 *From the Roman writer, Virgil*

Your task, Romans, is to rule the world. Establish civilisation where there is peace, be merciful when people surrender, destroy with war anyone who opposes you.

SOURCE 2 *Written by Cecil Rhodes, who was one of the leaders in building the British Empire in Africa in the late 1800s*

I contend that we are the first race in the world. And the more of the world we inhabit, the better it is for the human race. I will work for the furtherance of the British Empire, to bring the whole uncivilised world under British control.

SOURCE 3 *Written by Lord Curzon, the British viceroy [ruler] of India in 1900*

If I felt that we were not working here for the good of India … then I would see the link that holds England and India together broken without a sigh.

Into the Middle Ages

You are heading into the period of history called the Middle Ages and this first activity helps you to get your bearings. When were the Middle Ages and how do they fit in with the rest of the history you have studied?

Viking attacks on England from 790s to 1060s	Norman Conquest of England 1066

Roman Period – up to 400AD	Saxon Period c.400–1066	Middle Ages 1066–c.1500

1

a. Florence Nightingale improved nursing

c. The Black Death killed half the people of Europe

e. Gunpowder was used for the first time

b. Richard the Lionheart went on Crusade

d. The Industrial Revolution changed the way people earned their living

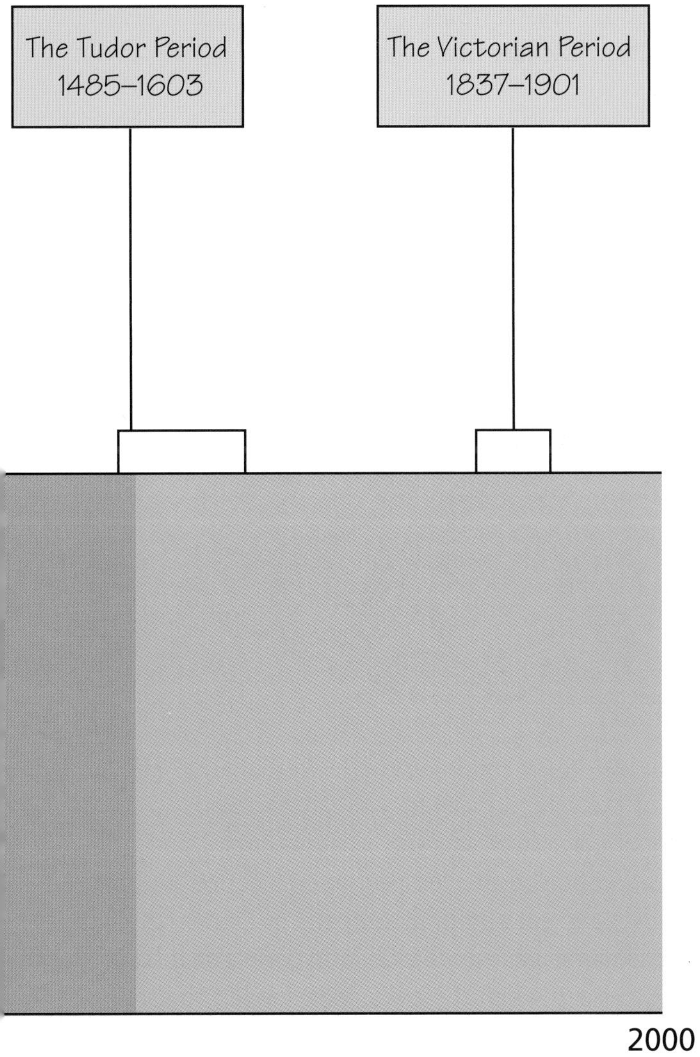

The Tudor Period
1485–1603
The Victorian Period
1837–1901
2000

ACTIVITY

1 Study the timeline and mark on your own copy anything that you have studied in Section 1.

2 The Norman Conquest of England started in 1066. Which century was 1066 in?

a) the tenth

b) the eleventh

c) the twelfth

3 Was the Middle Ages longer or shorter than the Saxon period?

4 Which of the events below do you think happened during the Middle Ages?
Your teacher can tell you if you are right.

h. The Spanish Armada was defeated

f. Elizabeth I was Queen of England

i. William the Conqueror won the Battle of Hastings

g. Books were printed for the first time in Europe

j. Peasants' Revolt: thousands of peasants marched to London to demand their rights

Into the mind of a medieval soldier!

There were many wars in the Middle Ages. There was a lot of peace as well but this section is about the wars, and the people who fought in them. You will begin by finding out about one very famous soldier, William Marshal. Why did he fight? Why did he risk his life?

The story of William Marshal

Hostage

William was only five years old when he **faced death** for the first time. In a civil war William's father promised to surrender his castle to King Stephen. To make sure he kept this promise, Stephen took five-year-old William as a hostage!

But William's father didn't keep his promise! He changed his mind and kept his castle. Stephen threatened to hang young William in revenge. William's father replied 'Hang him. I can always have more sons.'

Fortunately for William, King Stephen was a kind man and decided not to hang the child.

Trainee

From when he was seven or eight, the main focus of William's life was **learning to be a soldier**. He didn't do Maths, English, Geography or Science. He learned how to use a sword and a battle-axe, how to

ride a war-horse and be accurate with a lance. He did lots of exercise to make him as strong as possible. Becoming a soldier was the most important part of his education but he also learned how to dance, be polite to ladies and eat and drink properly at dinner (though his nickname was 'scoff-food' and people said he only went to sleep when there was nothing left to eat!).

When William grew up, there was a new king, Henry II. William quickly became known as a good soldier. He went on Crusade to capture Jerusalem. Perhaps that was where he learned one of his famous battle cries, 'By the sword of God'. He said that 'God helps the man who believes in him.'

Loyal

William was as well **known for his loyalty** as his skill with a sword. When King Henry's sons rebelled, William fought for Henry and knocked Prince Richard off his horse (and Richard is reckoned to be one of the greatest soldiers ever). William even stayed loyal to King John when most barons rebelled.

William said:

'By God's sword, if everyone else betrayed the King I would carry him on my shoulders and I would never fail him, even if it meant begging for my bread.'

And in 1216, when he was 70, William charged at the head of the royal army against an invading French army and led his side to victory!

Winner

Although he was a **brilliant soldier**, William did not take silly risks. He wanted to be a live winner, not a dead hero. He made sure that he had an excellent chance of winning before he led his men into battle. He believed it was better to win by trickery than die in a dramatic but pointless battle.

William developed his skills in tournaments. A tournament was a practice war. Knights took part in teams. They wore colours, had war cries and captains. The aim was to capture as many other knights as possible. When you captured a knight you won his horse and armour and he paid you a ransom (a sum of money) to be freed. Any tactic was allowed. Teams even hid in woods to ambush a knight or waited until everyone else was exhausted near the end of a tournament and then charged in. Although they were only 'practice', tournaments were still dangerous and many knights were killed in them.

In his career, William captured at least 500 knights, making money every time. In his best year, he and a knight called Roger captured 103 knights.

William was so successful because he used clever tactics and was extremely strong. He hit people harder and took more heavy blows than anyone else could survive. After one tournament William's helmet had been so knocked out of shape that he could not get it off so he found a blacksmith, who hammered it back into shape – with William's head still inside it!

Superstar

To people at the time, William was **the ideal knight**. He was a winner. He became an earl (the most senior position in England apart from being king) and owned land in Wales, Ireland and Normandy, as well as in England. He even governed the country for a while when the ten-year-old Henry III became King. He died rich, famous and respected by everyone.

ACTIVITY

1 What kind of man was William Marshal? Choose three words to describe his character.

2 Which of the following statements do you think William would be:
   a) most likely to say?
   b) least likely to say?

Make sure you can support your choice from the information given in the story.

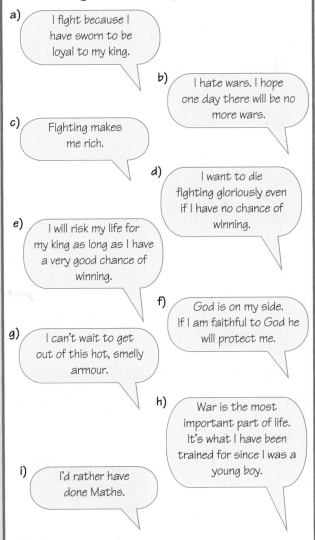

a) I fight because I have sworn to be loyal to my king.

b) I hate wars. I hope one day there will be no more wars.

c) Fighting makes me rich.

d) I want to die fighting gloriously even if I have no chance of winning.

e) I will risk my life for my king as long as I have a very good chance of winning.

f) God is on my side. If I am faithful to God he will protect me.

g) I can't wait to get out of this hot, smelly armour.

h) War is the most important part of life. It's what I have been trained for since I was a young boy.

i) I'd rather have done Maths.

3 What does the story of William Marshal tell you about war in the Middle Ages? Write down as many ideas as you can.

What questions do you want to ask about war?

You already know that one way of getting better at history is to ask good questions. On these two pages that is all you need to do – ask some interesting questions about war in the Middle Ages.

◀ SOURCE 1

▶ SOURCE 2

► **SOURCE 4**

ACTIVITY

Sources 1–4 were painted in the Middle Ages. They show different wars at different times.

1 Choose one picture and working on your own or with others write down as many questions as possible about your picture. You could do it like this:

You might ask about the detail, for example: 'Are these people prisoners?' or 'What's the soldier's armour made of?' Or you might ask questions that look behind the picture such as 'What are they fighting about?'

2 Swap your questions with someone else and see if you can add some more questions of your own about **their** picture. You could repeat

this for all the pictures if you have time.

3 Now go beyond the pictures. What other questions do you have about war in the Middle Ages? Write them down.

Together as a class:

4 You should now have lots of questions to choose from. From all these different questions people have asked, choose four or five that you think are really important, or interesting, or which are going to be particularly useful as you find out about war in the Middle Ages. These are your 'big questions'.

A quick history of war in the Middle Ages: who, when and why?

You can't study every medieval war in detail (and you probably would not want to) so here's a quick history of some of the main wars. Your task is to see the patterns: who won, who lost and why they were fighting!

ACTIVITY

Step 1 – understand your wars

Work in groups. Choose one colour of cards – green, blue or yellow.

Read all the cards for your group and get them into chronological (date) order.

Work out:

1 Who was fighting who?

2 What your wars were about.

3 Who won and who lost?

Step 2 – build a living graph

Still in groups.

4 Write the date and title of each war on a tabard like this:

5 Arrange your wars in date order.

6 Now put each tabard on a chart like this. You will need to decide where each event belongs on the Success/Failure line.

7 Take a digital photo of your graph.

1095
THE FIRST
CRUSADE

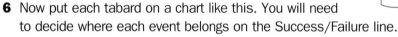

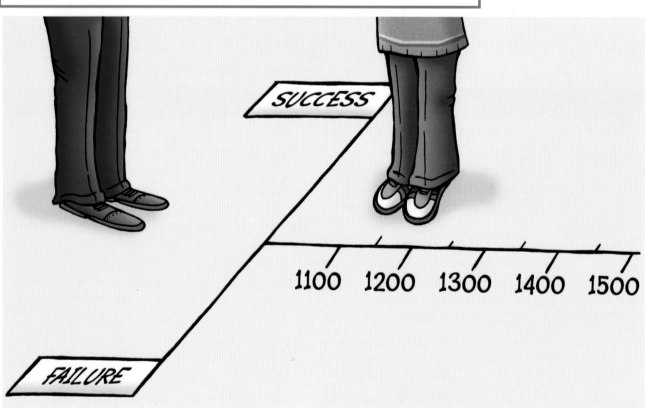

1204
King John lost all the English land in France to the King of France.

1270
Edward I, a great soldier, spent three years on Crusade but he could not win back Jerusalem.

1154
Henry II built up a huge empire. He was King of England and ruled half of France.

1187
The great Muslim general, Saladin, beat the Crusaders at the battle of Hattin and re-captured Jerusalem.

1380s
French soldiers landed in England and burned towns all along the south coast. This happened year after year.

1280s
Edward I wanted to control all of Britain. He conquered Wales and built great castles to keep control there.

1346
Edward III claimed that he was King of France and tried to conquer France. He won the Battles of Crécy and Poitiers but did not win the French crown.

1291
The last Crusader town in the Holy Land was captured by the Muslim army.

1314
Robert the Bruce, King of Scotland, beat the English army at Bannockburn, which ended the chances of England taking over Scotland for a long time.

1190
Richard I (the Lionheart) went on Crusade. He did win battles but never recaptured Jerusalem.

1290s
Edward I attacked the Scots (led by William Wallace), but was not able to take over Scotland completely.

1095
The First Crusade. Soldiers from Europe captured Jerusalem from Muslim control.

1403
Owain Glyn Dwr led a rebellion to force the English out of Wales. However, the Welsh were not strong enough and the rebellion failed.

1415
Battle of Agincourt: Henry V won a great victory over France and captured northern France.

1429
Joan of Arc became a French heroine when she led their army and pushed the English back. When the English caught Joan they burned her as a witch.

1453
The Battle of Castillon was a great French victory over the English, who lost all the lands Henry V had won. Only the town of Calais was still held by the English.

1171
Henry II invaded Ireland. He claimed he was King of Ireland although he only controlled a small part of it.

Who fought who? 1066 – the year of three battles

Now you are going to study one conflict in depth, the Norman Conquest of Britain. You'll find out why men risked their lives in this war, why the Normans won and how the war changed the lives of many, many people. You'll start with what happened in the famous year of 1066.

ACTIVITY

Tell the story of 1066 by making notes on your own copy of the map.

a) Which arrow shows the first army to invade England? Give it the number 1 and note down who was the leader and what happened.

b) Which arrow tells the next part of the story? Give it the number 2 and note down who was the leader and what happened.

c) Repeat this for the other arrows.

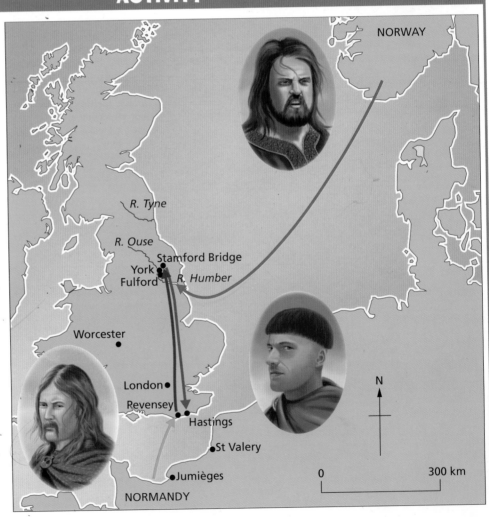

56

January — King Edward dies

Edward dies with no sons and there is confusion over who he wants to be the next king. Is it Harold the most powerful man in England, or William his friend from Normandy?

January — King Harold is crowned

At a grand ceremony in Westminster Abbey the English lords cheer. They swear loyalty to Harold as the only rightful King of England. The bishop declares that Harold is God's chosen king. Afterwards there is feasting and dancing.

Spring — William prepares

Across the English Channel, William (Duke of Normandy) is not surprised that Harold is now king but he is angry. He says the English crown had been promised to him. He tells his carpenters to build ships, and orders his knights to gather armies. He will invade England and fight Harold.

Spring — Hardrada prepares

In Norway there is yet another person who thinks he should be King of England. Harald Hardrada, King of Norway, gathers his own army too. His ancestors had been kings of England, so should he!

Summer — Harold's defence

King Harold knows an invasion is likely but not where or when. His earls Edwin and Morcar raise an army to defend the north against the Norwegians. Harold himself raises an army to defend the south. His loyal thegns bring their knights, archers and spearmen.

August — Harold's problem

Harold's army has been waiting all summer but nothing has happened. His soldiers are running out of food and many of his men have to go home to help with the harvest.

September — William's problem

William's army is ready, but he is stuck in Normandy. His boats can't sail because the wind is against him.

20th September — The Battle of Fulford

Five hundred Norwegian ships land in the north of England. Edwin and Morcar block their way but on 20 September the Norwegians beat the English army at the Battle of Fulford.

25th September — The Battle of Stamford Bridge

A messenger races from Yorkshire to give the news to King Harold. He immediately sets off, hastily reassembling his army, and rushes north at top speed. He travels so fast that he catches the Norwegians by surprise at Stamford Bridge, near York. He beats them convincingly.

28th September — The Normans land

King Harold and his army are still recovering when news comes that William has landed at Pevensey. William was lucky! The wind changed just when he needed it, while Harold was in the north.

Early October — Harold marches south

Harold sets off with his tired army. He gathers more troops on the way south.

14th October — The Battle of Hastings

In the early morning mist English and Normans face each other on a hillside near Hastings. The battle lasts all day. It is a close battle but finally King Harold is killed. The battle is over.

Christmas Day — King William I

William marches on London where the surviving English earls accept him as king. He is crowned King of England.

Why are they risking their lives at Hastings?

It is fairly obvious why King Harold and Duke William were fighting at the Battle of Hastings. One wanted to stay King of England and the other wanted to take over. It is less obvious why others might be there to join them. Let's find out.

ACTIVITY

1 Before you read this page, make a list of the reasons why you think people might come to fight at Hastings. Look back at what was in William Marshal's mind (pages 50–51).
2 Now read about the six characters on these pages and list all the reasons why they risked their lives in this battle.
3 Compare your lists. What are the similarities and differences between the motives of the Normans and the English?

1 Robert de Mortain
…is William's half brother. He comes from a family of soldiers; he has been trained to fight since he was young. Robert himself is a skilled horse rider and sword fighter. His family have always seized land from their neighbours by force whenever they have had the chance.

If William wins, Robert expects to be well rewarded with land.

2 Eolfric

…is a housecarl, part of Harold's own personal guard. Housecarls serve, protect and fight for the King. They are also the King's friends. Eolfric is prepared to fight to the death if necessary. Harold is a great leader and he wins all his battles. Eolfric believes that Harold is the rightful King of England. Harold was chosen by Edward and Eolfric thinks William's claim to be king is just an excuse to steal England.

3 Thorold
…is an English foot soldier. He is a local man from Sussex. Like every other man he has practised every week with bow and weapons since he was twelve years old. He doesn't get paid. It's just his duty to defend his country. He has come to Hastings because his lord told him to. The lord chose the men he trusts to obey orders, and not to panic.

Thorold is not expecting to fight. That will be done by the King's housecarls and the lords. Thorold is a reserve. He expects to spend more time talking about the harvest they've just brought in.

4 Godric …is an English thegn (a lord). He is the sheriff in Berkshire where he holds good land given to him by Harold. As sheriff he is the King's representative in the county, raising money for him and getting richer himself. If Harold loses, Godric knows the Normans will take his land, so he must fight to defend it. He does not want to end up a poor labourer working for a Norman lord. If Harold wins, Godric can expect some extra rewards.

5 Eustace …is the son of a Norman knight. However he is fourth son so will not inherit any land. The only way he can get riches is to follow his lord, Robert de Mortain. Back in Normandy he gets a small wage from Mortain and is given food, a horse and weapons, and a place to sleep in his castle. In return Eustace guards Robert's lands and fights for him in local wars.

If they win and Eustace fights well – Robert will reward Eustace by making him lord of a village. In time he might become richer than his older brothers. He will also be allowed to keep anything he can take from the dead and wounded enemies.

6 Hugh …carries the most important banner in William's army. The banner announces that the Pope has blessed William's campaign. The Pope has called it a holy crusade to get rid of Harold so it shows that God is on the Norman side.

Was England worth fighting for in 1066?

According to a trader who visited England in the eleventh century:

You can find all the riches of the world in England. On all sides are fields full of food, cattle and sheep and good warhorses. The rivers teem with fish and the wine they make is as good as in France. They weave beautiful cloth and there are rich metals – copper, iron, lead, tin, silver and gold.

Whose story does the Bayeux Tapestry tell?

You are now going to look at the Battle of Hastings through pictures. They come from the Bayeux Tapestry, the most famous account of the Battle of Hastings. Your task is to work out whose story it tells: the Norman version or the English version?

use an evidence frame

Put your picture in the centre of a very large sheet of paper like this to make your evidence frame.

● In the inner box write **information** you can see in the picture – what it definitely tells you.
● The middle box is for your inferences – an **inference** is more than a guess. It is something you can work out from the picture even if it is not shown.
● The outside box is for your **questions** – things you would like to know but which this picture does not tell you.

QUESTIONS I'd like to know:

INFERENCES I can work out that:

INFORMATION This definitely tells me that:

▼ SOURCE 1
A scene from the Bayeux Tapestry.

The Bayeux Tapestry was probably made for William's brother, Odo, the Bishop of Bayeux. It is about 75 yards long and 20 inches high.

A scene from the Bayeux Tapestry.

ACTIVITY

1 Look closely at Source 1. Your question is: What does this picture tell you about the Battle of Hastings?

2 The sentences below go in the boxes on the evidence frame. Put each sentence where you think it belongs, in the correct box.

3 Now add more sentences or questions of your own to each box.

The soldiers were well trained.

What is this flag for?

Soldiers wore helmets and a kind of armour.

A lot of people were killed or wounded.

Did both sides have cavalry?

They had shields and fought with spears and axes.

What other weapons did they use? Did they have guns?

This scene is quite late in the battle because there are so many dead.

Some soldiers fought on horseback.

Who are the dead people? Are they Norman or English?

It was woven in England within a few years of 1066 but it was planned and designed by Normans.

ACTIVITY

Now that you have practised looking closely at the Bayeux Tapestry, use those skills to work out whose side the tapestry is on – the Normans or the English.

1 Match each picture to one of these captions:

a) Norman soldiers set fire to a house that they have captured.

b) Harold is killed.

c) Harold is crowned king by Archbishop Stigand who had been told to stop carrying out services by the Pope.

d) Harold swears an oath to support Duke William's claim to the English throne.

e) Norman troops panic thinking William is dead. But William bravely rallies his troops and leads them on a charge.

f) A comet is seen in the sky. It frightens people who think it is a sign of an invasion to come.

g) Norman soldiers gather food from the English countryside to feed themselves as they prepare for the Battle of Hastings.

h) Harold rescues a Norman soldier.

2 Which two pictures most suggest:

a) the tapestry is on the Norman side?

b) the tapestry is on the English side?

4

HIC:EST:VVAD AR D:

5

:HAROLDO: REGIS

HIC RE SIDET HAROLD
REX:AN GLORVM:

STIGANT
ARCHIEPS

6

MV: TENENS: CONFOR: HICEST: WILE DUX: HIC FRAN

IVS

TAT PVE ROS

7

DE ARENA

8

ISTI MIRANT STELLA

HAROLD

Who told the truth about 1066?

Each side told the story of 1066 in its own way. The Normans wanted people to believe their version. The English wanted people to believe theirs. On pages 64–69 you can investigate both sides thoroughly and then decide who told the truth about the Battle of Hastings.

ACTIVITY

1 Work with a partner. Choose one of the monks John or Guillaume – not one monk each, one monk between you. Discuss how you think your monk might have answered the questions in their bubbles. Write down your main ideas.

2 Team up with another pair who have chosen the other monk and compare your answers to question 1. Identify:
  a) things that you disagree about
  b) things that you agree about.

3 Make a draft list of the reasons why the histories written by John and Guillaume might be different.

Now turn over and find out what John and Guillaume really wrote!

Meet John

John was an English monk who lived in the monastery at Worcester. He wrote a history of England about 70 years after 1066. He took his information from other English accounts that had been written earlier.

1 What do I want people to think of Harold?

2 What do I want people to think of William?

3 Which events in 1066 should I write most about?

4 Which events in 1066 should I leave out altogether?

Many sources

For some topics in the Middle Ages there are very few sources. War is different. People wrote a lot about wars and they made lots of pictures of war. So even though it happened nearly 1000 years ago there is a surprising amount of information about the Battle of Hastings – although you have to be careful using the sources because they are usually very one-sided.

1 Why do you think there are many sources about war? Think of as many reasons as you can.

2 Why do you think sources about war are likely to be one-sided?

Why monks?

You are going to compare the histories of the Battle of Hastings written by two monks. Many of the written sources from the Middle Ages were written by monks. This may surprise you, but monks were the professional writers of their time. Unlike today not many people could read or write so it was the monks who did the writing. Sometimes monks just wrote down what others told them to say. At other times they were like researchers, historians and journalists all rolled into one.

3 Why do you think monks learned to read and write in the Middle Ages?

4 Why do you think so few other people learned to read or write at this time?

1 What do I want people to think of Harold?

2 What do I want people to think of William?

3 Which events in 1066 should I write most about?

4 Which events in 1066 should I leave out altogether?

Meet Guillaume

Guillaume was a monk who lived at the abbey of Jumièges in Normandy, France. He wrote a history of the Dukes of Normandy in 1070. He probably spoke to men who were at Hastings, including William himself who visited Jumièges in 1067.

The evidence of John of Worcester

1 1066 – King Edward, after ruling England for twenty-three years, died at London on the eve of the Epiphany. He was buried the next day, amidst tears from all who were there. After King Edward was buried, the chief men of all England chose as king, Harold, son of Earl Godwin, whom King Edward had chosen before his death as his successor. He was crowned on the same day by Aldred, Archbishop of York. King Harold made good laws, helped churches and monasteries and ordered the arrest of all thieves and robbers. In that year, on 24 April, a comet was seen in the sky, blazing brightly for seven days.

2 During the summer, King Harold went to the Isle of Wight with his navy because William, Duke of the Normans (a cousin of King Edward) was preparing to invade England with an army. Harold watched all summer and autumn for his arrival, placing his army at strategic places around the coast. However, towards the nativity of St Mary, because food was running out, both the navy and army returned home.

3 After this, Harald Fairhair, King of the Norwegians, landed unexpectedly at the mouth of the River Tyne with an extremely strong fleet, more than 500 great ships. Earl Tostig, King Harold's brother, joined him and they sailed to the River Humber and up the River Ouse, landing at a place called Riccall. When King Harold heard this, he speedily marched north but before the King arrived, Earls Edwin and Morcar, with a great army, fought the Norwegians on the north bank of the River Ouse near York, on Wednesday the eve of St Matthew the Apostle's day. The English fought bravely but could not withstand the attacks of the Norwegians and fled after suffering many casualties. The Norwegians were victorious.

4 But five days later, on Monday 25 September, King Harold, with many thousands of well-armed soldiers, marched to York and fought the Norwegians at a place called Stamford Bridge. He killed Harald Fairhair and Tostig and the greater part of their army and gained total victory. King Harold thought his enemies had been defeated but then he was told that Duke William had landed his fleet at a place called

Pevensey with a huge number of mounted soldiers, archers and foot soldiers. Immediately King Harold marched his army to London in great haste. He knew that many of the bravest Englishmen had fallen in the two battles in the north and that half his army had not had time to assemble, yet he was not afraid to march against his enemy as quickly as he could. On Saturday 22 October, before a third of his army were ready, he joined battle with the Normans nine miles from Hastings, where he had built a castle.

5 But because the English were lined up in a narrow place many slipped away from the battlefield and very few remained true to the King. However, from the third hour of daylight until dusk he fought most bravely. But, when very many had died on both sides, King Harold himself was killed, alas. Earls Gyrth and Leofwine, his brothers, and the most of the noblemen of England were also killed.

6 Then Duke William returned to Hastings. King Harold had reigned nine months and as many days.

ACTIVITY

1 Read paragraphs 1 and 2 on page 66.
  a) John wanted to show that Harold was the **rightful** king. Which two pieces of information did he include to show this?
  b) What did John say to show that Harold was a **good** king?
2 Read paragraphs 3 and 4.
  a) How strong was the Norwegian army? Choose at least two details.
  b) What impression of King Harold of England do you get from paragraphs 3 and 4?
  c) John wrote as much about the Norwegian invasions as he did about William's invasion. Why do you think he wrote so much about the Norwegians?
3 Why do you think John did not write anything about William's preparations for invading England?
4 Read paragraphs 5 and 6. What reasons does John give to explain why the Normans won at Hastings?
5 John got the date of the Battle of Hastings wrong.
  a) What was the real date? (See page 57.)
  b) Why do you think he made this mistake about such an important event?
6 Think about what John wrote. Choose **two** words to describe how he felt about 1066. Which phrases from his history would you choose to support your answer?

The evidence of Guillaume of Jumièges

1 By the will of God, Edward, King of the English, had no heir, so he had sent Robert, Archbishop of Canterbury, to Duke William to appoint him heir to the kingdom of England. Later he also sent Harold, the most powerful English earl, to confirm the promise that Duke William would become King of England and to swear his loyalty to the Duke. However at the beginning of his mission, Harold was captured by Guy, Count of Abbeville, who threw Harold and his men into prison. When Duke William heard this he sent messengers ordering Guy to set Harold free. Then Harold stayed with Duke William and promised his loyalty to William as King of England.

2 At last King Edward died in the year of the Lord, 1065. Harold immediately seized the Kingdom, breaking the promises he had sworn to Duke William. The Duke sent messengers to Harold, urging him not to break his word but Harold would not listen and turned all the English people against the Duke. At that time a star appeared, its three-forked tail lighting up the southern sky for fifteen days. Many said it was a sign of a great change in the kingdom.

3 Duke William saw how Harold increased his power each day. Therefore the Duke hastily built a fleet of 3000 ships. The ships were anchored at Saint-Valery and filled with mighty horses and strong men armed with hauberks and helmets. Then, blown by a favourable wind, he crossed the sea and landed at Pevensey where he immediately built a castle. He left some troops in charge of it and speedily moved on to Hastings where he built another castle. Harold, hurrying to take Duke William by surprise, gathered a huge army and rode through the night, arriving at the battlefield at dawn.

4 The Duke had taken precautions against a night attack. At first light, he arranged his army in three divisions and without any fear advanced against the dreadful enemy. The battle began at the third hour and the slaughter continued until the late evening. Harold, fighting in the front rank of his army, died covered in wounds. When the English heard of their king's death, they fled.

ACTIVITY

1 Use your own copy of this table to compare what John and Guillaume wrote about 1066. We have filled out John's section for you. Read paragraphs 1–4 on page 68, then fill out Guillaume's section.

Topic	John of Worcester, the Englishman	Guillaume of Jumièges, the Norman
a) Who Edward wanted to be king	King Edward chose Harold and so did the chief men of England. He was crowned by the Archbishop of York.	
b) The Norwegian invasion and battles	Harold quickly and bravely defeated the Norwegians. John wrote as much about it as about William's invasion.	
c) William's preparations and invasion	John did not mention preparations. He only wrote a few words about the landing.	
d) Where the battle took place and how long it lasted	Nine miles from Hastings; it lasted all day.	
e) Strength of the English army	Harold had lost soldiers in the northern battles. He fought before a third of his men were ready. Some deserted Harold.	
f) William's tactics	Not mentioned at all.	
g) How Harold died	Harold fought bravely and was killed late in the battle. No details about how he was killed.	

2 What impression of Harold do you get from paragraphs 1 and 2? Choose at least two phrases to support your answer.

3 Guillaume does not mention the Norwegian invasion and the battles in the north. Why do you think he left them out?

4 What impression do paragraphs 3 and 4 give you of William as a leader?

5 Think about what Guillaume wrote. Choose **two** words to describe how he felt about 1066. Which phrases from his history would you choose to support your answer?

On page 65 you predicted what the monks would say and why they might disagree. Look back at your predictions. What have you learned since then?

DOING HISTORY: Evidence

Using sources well means

…identifying why sources don't always tell the whole truth

Why didn't John and Guillaume tell the whole truth?

I wanted to praise …

I didn't know about …

I was ashamed so I …

I wanted to persuade people that …

John the Englishman   **Guillaume the Norman**

1. John and Guillaume's thought bubbles give reasons why they didn't tell the whole truth. Can you match the endings A–F to the correct starters and the correct person?

> **Endings**
> A …Harold's plans for defending the coast during the summer.
> B …Harold was a good king despite being defeated.
> C …William's preparations. It was a long time ago and I wasn't there.
> D …didn't write much about the English losing the battle of Hastings.
> E …William because he has given a lot of money to our Abbey.
> F …William was the true king and not just an invader.

2. If a writer doesn't tell the truth about one thing, does it mean that you can't trust anything he or she says? Think about John and Guillaume's writing to help you with this.

70

Using sources well means

...using a variety of sources

It would be neat and convenient if there were one source in history that told you the whole story, truthfully and clearly, but that is rarely the case. In most situations you need to use a range of sources to build your picture of events or periods.

3 Make a list of the kinds of sources that give us evidence about 1066.

4 List two kinds of things that the Bayeux Tapestry tells you about the Battle of Hastings that the written sources on pages 66–68 do not.

Using sources well means

... knowing how certain you are

We can't always find **definite** answers in History because often:

- we don't have enough sources
- they don't tell us everything we want to know
- they disagree with each other.

Therefore when you work out an answer to an enquiry you need to say **how definite** your answer is.

5 List two things **we know for certain** about the events of 1066.

6 List two things **we cannot be certain** of about the events of 1066.

LEARNING LOG

What are the most important things you have learned from John and Guillaume about using sources? How are you going to record them?

On Christmas Day 1066 William was crowned King of England but that did not mean he controlled the country. There is a difference between winning a battle and conquering a country. There were two million English but only 10,000 Normans. So what happened next? How did the Normans conquer England?

'A fatal day!'

One English monk wrote that William's victory at the Battle of Hastings was 'a fatal day. Now we are ruled by foreigners and strangers'. Another monk said that the Normans had 'stolen England and robbed the people'. These two pages explain why.

Land

William rewarded his supporters by giving them English land. In return for land they promised to provide soldiers whenever William needed them. For example, Robert de Montain, William's half-brother was given 793 manors (villages). This made him the second largest landowner in England (after William himself). Many English lords lost their land and now had to work for French lords.

Castles

The Normans built castles to protect their soldiers. The first castles were made of wood so they were quick to build and good for defence. Soon they were building stone castles that towered above the surrounding towns.

Between 1066 and 1087, the Normans built around 100 castles, mostly in towns. The Normans destroyed many houses to make way for their castles, and forced the English to build them.

▲ SOURCE 1
A drawing of a typical, wooden Norman castle.

Hunting laws

The Normans stopped the English hunting in their forests. Hunting was not just a sport in those days, it was an important way of getting food. The punishment for people caught hunting in the royal forests was to have two fingers cut off. The punishment for a second offence was to have your eyes gouged out.

Language

The King and his men spoke Norman French. The ordinary people carried on speaking English. The difference in language made them afraid as they did not know what their lords were saying.

Churches

Saxon churches and cathedrals were knocked down to make way for bigger, grander Norman ones. These showed off the Normans' wealth and power as well as being places of worship.

▲ **SOURCE 2**
Durham cathedral, built by the Normans.

▲ **SOURCE 3**
Norman soldiers gathering food from the English countryside.

ACTIVITY

Tabloid newspapers are a modern invention but if one had existed in the eleventh century, how would they have covered these events? Use the stories and evidence on these two pages to create your own tabloid newspaper.

THE ENGLISH NEWS
FATAL DAY!

Rebellions 1067–1070

Not surprisingly, the English did not take all this lying down. This map shows the rebellions faced by the Normans 1067–1070.

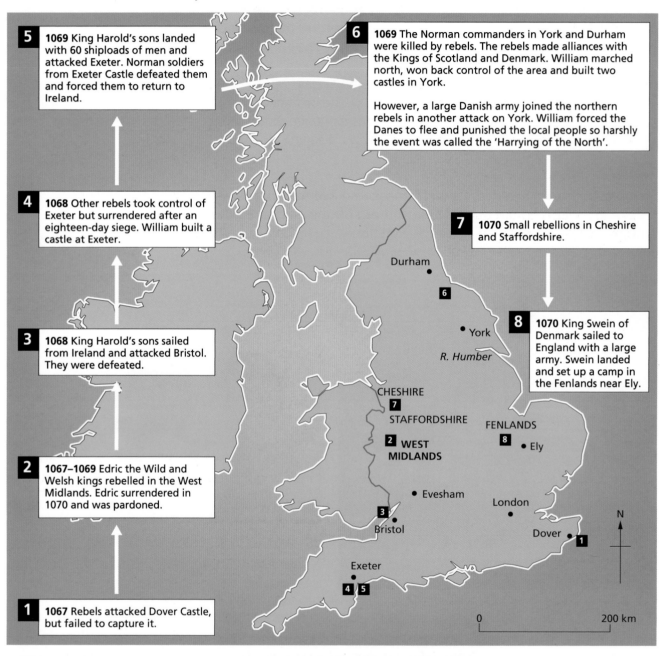

5 1069 King Harold's sons landed with 60 shiploads of men and attacked Exeter. Norman soldiers from Exeter Castle defeated them and forced them to return to Ireland.

6 1069 The Norman commanders in York and Durham were killed by rebels. The rebels made alliances with the Kings of Scotland and Denmark. William marched north, won back control of the area and built two castles in York.

However, a large Danish army joined the northern rebels in another attack on York. William forced the Danes to flee and punished the local people so harshly the event was called the 'Harrying of the North'.

4 1068 Other rebels took control of Exeter but surrendered after an eighteen-day siege. William built a castle at Exeter.

7 1070 Small rebellions in Cheshire and Staffordshire.

3 1068 King Harold's sons sailed from Ireland and attacked Bristol. They were defeated.

8 1070 King Swein of Denmark sailed to England with a large army. Swein landed and set up a camp in the Fenlands near Ely.

2 1067–1069 Edric the Wild and Welsh kings rebelled in the West Midlands. Edric surrendered in 1070 and was pardoned.

1 1067 Rebels attacked Dover Castle, but failed to capture it.

Durham

York

R. Humber

CHESHIRE **7**

STAFFORDSHIRE

FENLANDS

8 • Ely

2 WEST MIDLANDS

• Evesham

London

3 •
Bristol

Dover **1**

Exeter •
4 **5**

N

0   200 km

ACTIVITY 1

1 Did the English benefit or suffer from being ruled by William? Place topics from pages 72–81, such as castles and rebellions, on this line to build up a summary of the effects of the Norman Conquest.

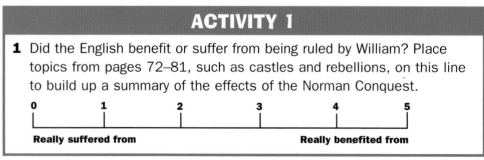

0   1   2   3   4   5

Really suffered from   Really benefited from

The Harrying of the North

The Normans severely punished anyone who rebelled against them. The worst case of all was the Harrying of the North (number 6 on the map). This is what happened according to a Norman monk who wrote a history of this time.

King William ordered officers to repair the castles in York. He himself combed the forests and hills, determined to hunt out the enemy hidden there. He killed many people, destroyed the camps of others, harried the land and burned homes to ashes. Nowhere else had William been so cruel. He punished the innocent as much as the guilty. In his anger he commanded that all crops and herds of animals, property and food should be burned so that the whole region north of the Humber would be stripped of all ways of making a living. As a result, a terrible famine fell on the people so that more than 100,000 people died of hunger. I have often praised William before, but for this act, which killed innocent as well as guilty by slow starvation, I cannot support him.

The word 'harry' means to ravage or destroy. Many English people became refugees as they fled from the soldiers and later from famine. Records show for example that some turned up at the abbey of Evesham, 120 miles away, where they were helped by monks.

If you were an English person at this time how would you have felt?

ACTIVITY 2

2 Add another page to your tabloid newspaper to describe the events on these two pages.

3 Discuss: Why do you think William punished people in the North so severely?

What should Hereward do?

Hereward came from a wealthy family living near Peterborough. He was short-tempered. He got into trouble at home in 1063 so went abroad where he became a soldier. He came back to England after 1066. He soon had a decision to make.

In 1070 King William ordered his soldiers to search for money and treasures hidden by rebellious Englishmen. At Peterborough Abbey the monks were worried that the Norman soldiers would take the abbey's treasures too, especially as William had just chosen a new abbot. The new man in charge was called Turold. He was a Norman (of course) and he was more of a soldier than a churchman. Turold was on his way to Peterborough with 160 soldiers.

Hereward knew the monks at Peterborough well. His uncle had been the last English abbot at Peterborough.

> What should I do now: resist or keep quiet?

ACTIVITY

1 On the opposite page are some of the factors that will affect Hereward's decision. Work with a partner. Sort the factors on a decision line like this.

Resist   **Keep quiet**

2 Which of the following options do you advise Hereward to take?
   a) Promise loyalty to William and hope for rewards.
   b) Leave the country and seek your fortune elsewhere.
   c) Fight William to save the abbey's treasures.
   d) Don't make a fuss. Try to live quietly.

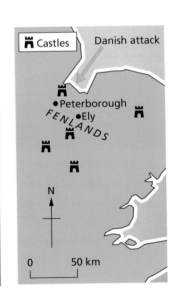

Castles   Danish attack

Peterborough
Ely
FENLANDS

N

0   50 km

1 The Normans have been taking away English land and giving it to their own people. Your land may be next.

2 The Normans want the abbey treasures. You feel that the gold is part of your heritage, your history.

3 The Danes have arrived in England. They could be good allies because they are a strong fighting force.

4 The Danes are famous for treachery. They are only interested in money.

5 William is always worried that his enemies back in Normandy will seize his land and property while he is away. He really needs to spend more time in Normandy.

6 There have been many rebellions against the Normans. None has succeeded.

7 The last rebellion in the north of England really worried William. In revenge he 'harried' the north; 100,000 people died in the famine that followed.

8 Ely is a really secure place, surrounded by marshes. You know it well but the Normans will take weeks to find a path through it.

9 You are not famous in England People won't be flocking to help you. But at least the people of Ely know you and your family.

10 You have three years' experience as a warrior. That's not much but you think you are a good one.

11 A successful rebellion would need to be planned and co-ordinated and involve other regions.

12 William was been crowned King of England by the Archbishop – God's representative on earth. Some say he was the great King Edward's chosen successor anyway.

13 There are castles everywhere and they are packed with Norman soldiers. Wherever you go you will have to deal with those castles.

14 There are rumours that other English lords are joining the Danes to fight William.

What happened next?

1 Hereward decided to take the abbey's treasures to stop them falling into Norman hands.

2 With the help of the Danes, he raided Peterborough Abbey. In the attack, the monastery buildings and people's homes in the town were burned down.

3 Hereward took the abbey's gold, silver and jewelled ornaments back to the Isle of Ely and hid them in the Danish ships!

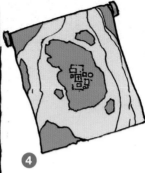

4 Ely was a large island, about twelve miles long by ten miles wide, surrounded by rivers, mud banks and marshes. It was a good base for the rebels and they stayed there, coming out to attack Norman soldiers.

5 William was determined to end this rebellion quickly. The Danes were a menace and he wanted to go home to Normandy to deal with trouble there. William sent messengers to King Swein offering him money if the Danes would go home. Bribery worked!

6 The Danes had only ever been interested in financial gain, and they sailed home with William's money as well as the treasures from Peterborough Abbey that had been left in their ships! The treasures were put in a Danish church. Hereward and his men were left alone to fight William.

7 Next, William surrounded the Isle of Ely but he had to find some way of crossing the waters and marsh. He ordered his men to build a causeway out of wood, stones, trees and even inflated cowhides, hoping that his knights could ride across this bridge.

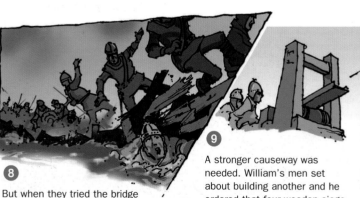

8 But when they tried the bridge collapsed under the weight. Men in chainmail armour and their horses drowned in the marsh.

9 A stronger causeway was needed. William's men set about building another and he ordered that four wooden siege towers be built. On top were catapults which hurled stones at Hereward's men to stop them attacking the bridge builders.

11 The new bridge was much more successful. It was made by tying small boats together and covering them with wooden planks. This proved much stronger and William's cavalry crossed onto Ely.

10 William also sent a woman, who was said to be a witch, up one of the towers to scream curses at the rebels. The rebels attacked the towers and set them on fire. The witch fell, breaking her neck.

⑫

The fighting did not last long. William promised that anyone who stopped fighting would be fairly treated, so many surrendered. Some managed to escape, including Hereward who was never heard of again. Perhaps he went back to Europe, fighting for whoever paid him the most money.

⑬

William broke his word. He imprisoned the lords who had joined the rebellions but treated others more harshly. Some rebels had their hands or feet cut off, others had their eyes put out. This was William's warning to anyone else who was considering rebellion.

⑭

Once William had got rid of the Danes there were no more major rebellions by the English. William had won. Between 1066 and 1072 he had spent most of his time in England but from 1072 to his death in 1087 he spent very little time there.

ACTIVITY 1

Why did Hereward fail?
These four Norman knights are discussing why Hereward's rebellion failed. How might they complete their word bubbles?

ACTIVITY 2

Was Hereward right or wrong to rebel?
Write a paragraph explaining what you think. Use the words in the box to help you.

hero	rescue	rebel	traitor	resist	loyal	cruel
		freedom	trick	brave		

Think about:
- Did he rebel for a good reason?
- Did he have much chance of success?
- Was he right to risk his own and other people's lives?
- Should he have accepted William as king?
- Should he have trusted the Danes to help?

Hereward is not a …

The rebels don't …

The Danes just want …

The English are frightened of …

William the ... what?

After William died the Normans called him William the Conqueror and the name has stuck. What do you think the English would have called him? Your task is to choose a name and then write an obituary (a description of his life) to go with it.

William dies

In 1087 King William died fighting. He had just captured a French town but, as he rode in triumph through the streets, a spark of burning wood fell beneath his horse's hooves. The frightened horse reared up, throwing William back and then violently forward. The iron pommel on his saddle drove into his stomach, injuring him so badly that he died a few days later. As soon as William died, servants stole his jewels and clothes, leaving his body naked. Worse was to come. At his funeral, the coffin was too small for his swollen body. As men tried to force his body into the coffin, it burst, causing a terrible stink. The nobles and bishops ran out of the cathedral, leaving a handful of monks to bury the King.

After William died many English people wrote about his life. Here are a few of them.

SOURCE 1 *A monk wrote this in the* Anglo-Saxon Chronicle

King William was greater and stronger than all the kings before him. He was kind to the good monks who served God. During his reign, the great cathedral at Canterbury was built and so were many others. He was cruel to anyone who disobeyed him, putting lords and even his own brother in prison. He kept good order in the country. A man with a bag of gold could travel unharmed right through the country. No man dared to kill another.

▲ SOURCE 2
William as shown in the Bayeux Tapestry.

SOURCE 3 A description of the Domesday survey by a monk

The King sent his men all over England, into every shire and had them find out how much land the king, the bishops and the lords had in each county and how much that land was worth. So very detailed was this investigation that there was no land, no ox, no cow, no sheep nor one pig left out (I am ashamed to write this but he was not ashamed to do it), and all these records were brought to him.

What was the Domesday Book?

The information in Domesday Book was collected in 1086. William wanted to know exactly who owned each village and what each village was worth. He wanted this information to help him collect more taxes and to feed his soldiers if the Danes threatened to invade England again. He sent officials round the country to ask very detailed questions. Then he sent another group of officials to check the answers were correct. The Domesday Survey covered all of England except Cumbria, Durham and Northumberland. Source 4 is an example of what they found.

SOURCE 4 From Exon Domesday book

Lands of the abbot of Tavistock in Devon

On the lands of the manor of Tavistock are 37 villeins and other householders, 12 slaves, 1 horse, 26 cattle, 12 pigs, 200 sheep, 30 goats. The manor is worth 12 pounds a year to the abbot.

Six knights hold land from the abbot. On Hugh's land are 1 villein and 6 other villagers, 2 slaves, 7 ploughing oxen, 10 cattle, 12 pigs and 60 sheep.

SOURCE 5 An English poem about William

The king was a tough and greedy man.
He forced the poor to build castles.
He took many gold coins from his people
And many more hundreds of pounds in
    silver.
He marked out huge forests for deer and
    made laws about hunting.
Anyone who killed a deer was to be blinded.
He loved the stags as dearly
As if he was their father.
The rich complained and the poor wept
But he was too merciless to care if everyone
    hated him.
They had to obey him.
Or they lost their lives and their lands,
Their goods and the king's friendship.

ACTIVITY

Details that praise William	Details that criticise William

1 Use Sources 2–5 and anything else you have studied in this section to fill out the chart above. Use one colour for details recorded by English writers and another for details recorded by Normans.

2 Now choose a nickname for William instead of '…the Conqueror'. For example, you might want to call him 'William the Ruthless' or 'William the Strong'.

3 Why might the English and the Normans disagree about a nickname for William?

4 After someone famous dies the newspapers often print an obituary, which summarises important things about the person's life and gives a judgement on their successes and failures. Write a paragraph to sum up William. Before you start, decide whether you are writing from the English or the Norman point of view.

A quick history of castles, weapons and armour

How did castles change?

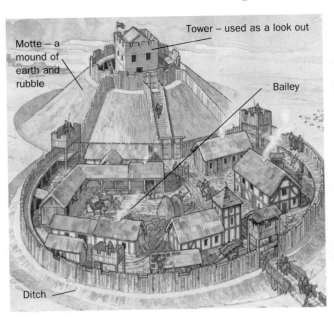

Motte – a mound of earth and rubble

Tower – used as a look out

Bailey

Ditch

Entrance on the second floor defended by gatehouse and drawbridge

Small windows

Eight storeys high

Curtain wall

Eleventh century

An artist's impression of a typical motte and bailey castle. When they conquered England in 1066 the Normans quickly built many simple castles like this. There was usually a wooden tower on top of a mound called a motte. Most mottes were less than 5 metres high. Next to the motte was the bailey (which varied in shape and size) where the soldiers lived, stored their weapons and stabled their war horses.

1 a) Why do you think the Normans built their first castles out of wood?
   b) Why were castles rebuilt in stone?

2 a) What does the story of the siege of Rochester tell you about the weaknesses of square keeps?
   b) How could you solve this weakness?

Twelfth century

In the twelfth century, most motte and bailey castles were rebuilt in stone. At the centre was the strongest part of the castle called the keep, where the soldiers and lord lived. This keep at Rochester castle was built in 1127. It was the biggest in the country. It withstood all attacks until a siege in 1215 (see panel).

The siege of Rochester 1215

One hundred rebel knights defended the castle against King John's army for two months until the King used a secret weapon – pigs. Miners dug their way under one corner of the keep. They filled the hole with wood. Then 40 pigs were killed. Their fat was poured into the hole and set alight. The fat burned strongly, keeping the blaze going until all the wood was burned. As the wood collapsed, so did the corner of the keep above it. The King's men swarmed into the keep through the gap in the defences. The King had won!

Keep – walls up to 5 metres thick with corridors inside

Round towers – hard to undermine

Three stage gatehouse

Moat

Large windows

Entrances on the ground floor on three sides

Brick walls

Thirteenth/fourteenth century

When Edward I set out to conquer Wales in 1276 he brought in the best castle builders from Europe to build strong castles where his soldiers would be safe from Welsh attacks. This one at Beaumaris was started in 1295. It had walls within walls so attackers who got through the outer defences then faced even stronger walls and towers. When the castle was in use the central area would have been full of buildings, supplies, people and animals.

Fifteenth century

England was much more peaceful. Tattershall castle was built in 1434. The owner knocked down a keep like the one at Rochester and replaced it with this brick tower to live in and entertain guests. It had wide staircases and wooden floors. By this time castles were mostly used as homes not as defences. Not even a castle was strong enough to withstand cannonballs.

3 What makes Beaumaris Castle harder to attack than Rochester?

4 How do the features labelled on the picture prove that Tattershall castle was built as a home rather than a defence?

5 Which period saw the biggest changes in castles? Support your answer by giving examples from these two pages or from your own research.

How did armour and weapons change?

Eleventh century

Thirteenth century

A Norman knight on horseback, with his shield and chainmail armour, could cut through enemy foot soldiers like a modern tank through soldiers on foot.

1. What changes in armour and weapons can you see between the eleventh and the thirteenth century?

2. Why do you think these changes took place?

3. Were these big changes or small changes?

Fourteenth century

The key weapon was now the longbow. Good archers could fire ten or twelve arrows a minute over a distance of 275 metres. It took years of training to become a good archer.

Knights began to wear plate armour rather than chainmail over the most vulnerable parts of their body but arrows could still pierce armour.

Knights preferred to fight on foot because their horses were too easy a target for the archers.

④ What changes in armour and fighting were caused by the longbow?

Fifteenth century

By the fifteenth century knights wore full plate armour if they could afford it. A knight in armour could still run, get onto his horse and get up if he was knocked over.

Weapons changed because of plate armour. Swords were more pointed so they could be thrust through gaps in armour and knights carried pole-axes (see picture above) which could cut through plate armour like a tin opener.

Gunpowder was first used in Europe in the 1300s. The first cannon were not very accurate, but by the fifteenth century they were more effective.

⑤ Why was the use of gunpowder an important development in warfare?

⑥ Which period saw the biggest changes in weapon and armour? Support your answer carefully with examples from these two pages or from your own research.

Why is the story of Henry V and Agincourt so popular?

One of the most famous battle in the Middle Ages took place at Agincourt. Ever since 1415 the story of the battle and its hero, Henry V, has been retold in books, plays and films. Can you see why it has always been a popular story – in England at least?

ACTIVITY

Read the story, then discuss these questions.

1 Why was the English army facing disaster in September 1415?
2 Which incident shows the French expected to win easily?
3 Pick out one incident you could use in a film to show Henry's heroism. Explain your choice.
4 Why did the English win against all the odds? (See if you can find at least three reasons.)
5 One part of this story is sometimes left out of English films. Which part, do you think? Why?
6 Why has this story been retold so often, especially when England has been at war?

▼ **SOURCE 1** *A modern re-enactor shows a longbow in action. In Henry V's time, the best archers could fire ten to twelve arrows a minute for a distance of 275 metres.*

▲ **SOURCE 2** *Henry V, King of England 1413–1422.*

Background

Henry had been leading armies since he was just sixteen. He became king when he was 26 and immediately began to plan an invasion of France. At first, the French weren't worried (even though the French king thought he was made of glass and would break if anyone touched him). They sent Henry a parcel of tennis balls as they thought he was more interested in sport and drinking than in war.

France, late September 1415

The English army was facing disaster. Two months previously, King Henry V had invaded France with 9,000 men. Henry wanted to be remembered as a great soldier so he planned to capture the town of Harfleur and beat the French in a great battle. He also hoped this would unite his lords who had been waging civil wars for twenty years.

The plan had gone badly wrong. It had taken a month to capture Harfleur. Two thousand English soldiers had died, many from disease. Henry had to decide what to do next. If he took his men home he would be a failure. If he marched across France and sailed home from Calais it would show the French he was not afraid. But what if their army caught the English, who were not fit to fight a major battle?

Early October 1415

King Henry decided to march across France. He led his army out of Harfleur on 8 October. He had 900 knights and 5,000 archers with food for eight days. All went well until they reached the River Somme. Then scouts brought news that the bridges over the river had been destroyed. Worse, a huge French army was on the other side.

Henry had to find another way to cross the river. They headed north until they found a place where the river was very shallow. It took several hours to get everyone across. Every minute the English expected the French to appear, ready for battle.

The English marched on, hungry, their food running out. Many were exhausted by illness. Somewhere nearby the French army waited.

24 October 1415

That evening the English made camp. They could see the huge French army in front of them. They were heavily outnumbered. An English knight, Sir Walter Hungerford, said to the King that he wished he had an extra 10,000 of the best archers in England. King Henry replied, 'That is foolish. I would not have a single man more. The men with me are God's people. God will help us overcome the French.'

The English expected to die the next day. They confessed their sins to God.

All night the French laughed, the knights gambling over the prisoners they would take.

25 October 1415, the Feast of Saints Crispin and Crispinian

King Henry chose a narrow battle line. There was woodland on both sides so the French could not ride round the sides of his army. He set out a line of knights with archers amongst them. Each archer hammered stakes into the ground to protect him from the charging French horses. They waited... but the French did not attack.

King Henry moved his men forward until they were just 180 metres from the French line. Then he ordered his archers to open fire. As the arrows fell, the French lost patience. They charged forward but, with the ground boggy after the heavy rain, their charge was slow. The English archers raised their bows and fired again and again, each man firing twelve arrows every minute. Sixty thousand arrows hammered down every minute onto the French knights and their horses.

The ground was covered in dead and wounded French knights and horses, but the bulk of the French had still not attacked. They moved forward on foot but stumbled over bodies, and frightened horses charged into them. Finally the two armies clashed in hand-to-hand fighting. The English were still heavily outnumbered but the battle had turned in their favour. The French could not make their numbers count because of the narrow battlefield. King Henry, in the thickest of the fighting, had his helmet broken by a blow from a French knight.

The English took hundreds of prisoners who were held at the back of the army. Then the King saw the French organising another attack. What if the prisoners broke free and attacked the English from the rear? Henry ordered his men to kill the prisoners. This was against the rules of war. It also meant losing large amounts of ransom money that would be paid by the prisoners' families. Henry's knights refused so he sent 200 archers to kill the prisoners. Nobody knows how many died.

The French counter-attack failed. The English had won. Between 7,000 and 10,000 Frenchmen were killed at the battle of Agincourt. Fewer than 30 English soldiers died. When the news reached England, there were great celebrations in London. Henry V and his archers had become English heroes.

What should everyone know about the Crusades?

You are now going to find out about a series of wars in Europe and the Middle East known as the Crusades. Your task will be to create a website that sums up what you think people should know about these wars.

ACTIVITY 1

Starter

Pictures 1–4 are all sources about the Crusades. What impression does each give you of the Crusades? Write a sentence to sum up the interpretation. Here are some words that you could use: hero, dangerous, noble, cruel, exciting…

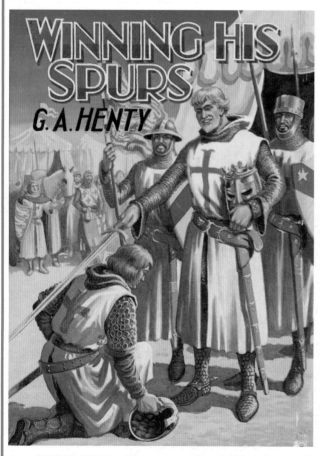

▲ **SOURCE 1** *The cover of a children's novel about the Crusades, first published in 1882.*

▲ **SOURCE 2** *A nineteenth-century engraving of the execution of Muslim prisoners, ordered by King Richard after the siege of Acre, 1191.*

▼ **SOURCE 3** *A statue of Saladin, a Muslim leader in the Crusades. The statue stands outside the city of Damascus in Syria where Saladin grew up.*

▼ **SOURCE 4** *A medieval drawing of a Crusader knight.*

ACTIVITY 2

Main task

Your main task over the next eight pages will be to work with others to create web pages that help people to understand the Crusades. You should make one page about each of the following topics:

● What were the Crusades and why was Jerusalem important? (use pages 90–91)
● Who were the Crusaders and why did they fight? (use pages 92–93)
● What were relationships like between Christians and Muslims? (use pages 94–95)
● Case study: King Richard or Saladin? (use pages 96–97).

You could work in groups and take one topic each or do all four.

ACTIVITY 3

Review tasks

1 After you have made your web pages, decide which of these speakers you most agree with and write a paragraph to explain why:

> We shouldn't study the Crusades at school because...

> We should study the Crusades at school because ...

2 Look back to your questions about war that you studied on pages 52–53. As a result of your work on the Crusades:

   a) do you want to add any more questions?

   b) do you have answers to some of your questions?

What were the Crusades?

ACTIVITY 1

Here's the answer many people would give to the question above:

> In the Crusades, Christians were trying to win back control of their holy city Jerusalem.

1 Study these two pages to check this answer. Look carefully at each part of the sentence.
  - Were all Crusades fought to control Jerusalem?
  - Was Jerusalem only a holy city for Christians?

2 Write a web page to give a better answer to the question 'What were the Crusades?'

▼ **SOURCE 5** *A map of Crusades 1095–1500s.*

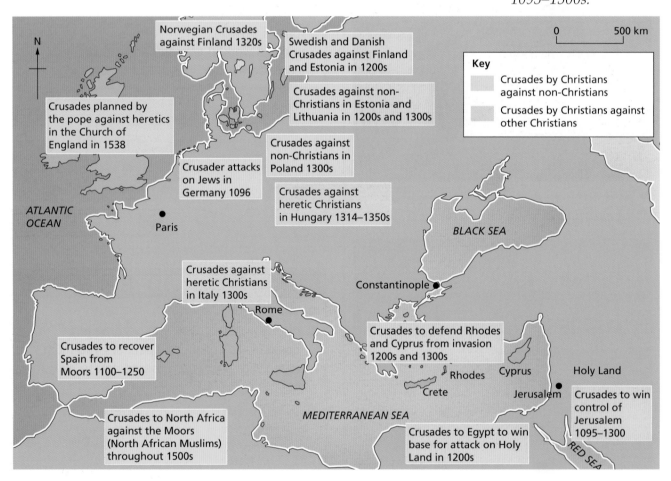

Norwegian Crusades against Finland 1320s

Swedish and Danish Crusades against Finland and Estonia in 1200s

Crusades against non-Christians in Estonia and Lithuania in 1200s and 1300s

Crusades planned by the pope against heretics in the Church of England in 1538

Crusades against non-Christians in Poland 1300s

Crusader attacks on Jews in Germany 1096

Crusades against heretic Christians in Hungary 1314–1350s

Key
- Crusades by Christians against non-Christians
- Crusades by Christians against other Christians

ATLANTIC OCEAN

Paris

BLACK SEA

Crusades against heretic Christians in Italy 1300s

Constantinople

Rome

Crusades to defend Rhodes and Cyprus from invasion 1200s and 1300s

Crusades to recover Spain from Moors 1100–1250

Rhodes   Cyprus   Holy Land

Crete

Jerusalem

Crusades to win control of Jerusalem 1095–1300

Crusades to North Africa against the Moors (North African Muslims) throughout 1500s

MEDITERRANEAN SEA

Crusades to Egypt to win base for attack on Holy Land in 1200s

RED SEA

0   500 km

Why was Jerusalem important?

One aim of the Crusades was to recapture Jerusalem from Muslim control. What was so important about Jerusalem?

Source 6 is a medieval Christian map of the world. Jerusalem is at the centre of the world because it was where Jesus Christ was crucified and rose again. These are the most important events in history according to Christian beliefs. In the Middle Ages Christians made pilgrimages to pray at the church of the Holy Sepulchre on the site where Jesus' body was buried and rose again. Christians called the whole area around Jerusalem 'the Holy Land' because it was where Jesus had lived.

◀ SOURCE 6 *Map of the world showing Jerusalem in the centre.*

ACTIVITY 2

Discuss
3 Why would studying the Crusades be dangerous if you:
 a) ignored all the Crusades in Europe against other kinds of Christians?
 b) ignored the fact that Jerusalem was a holy city for Muslims and Jews as well as for Christians?

Jerusalem was a holy city for others too.
* For Muslims it is the site from which the prophet of Islam – Muhammad – was taken up to Heaven. Pilgrims from Muslim countries went to pray there.
* For Jews it was the site of the holy temple built by King David which for centuries was the centre of Jewish worship. Even after the temple was destroyed, Jews regarded Jerusalem as a holy place.

91

Who were the Crusaders?

Many people went on Crusade because the Christian Church promised that anyone who died on Crusade would go straight to heaven (see Source 7) and avoid the horrors of hell (see Source 8). Also, the Pope was worried about the spread of violence in western Europe. Young men being trained for war were fighting each other. The Pope thought the Crusades might help this problem!

▼ **SOURCE 7** *Heaven painted on a wall in St Mary the Virgin Church, Bacton, Suffolk. It shows St Peter greeting the souls at the gates of Heaven.*

SOURCE 8 *A description of Hell by a monk in the 1300s*

In place of a scented bath there will be a bath black and foul. In place of a soft couch, they shall have a bed more painful and hard than all the nails in the world. Instead of wives they shall have toads. Their body shall have a throng of worms. They shall have eternal torment.

Here's the answer many people would give to the question above left:

> Crusaders were soldiers who were very religious.

Study these two pages and:

1 Make a list of all the different types of people who went on Crusade.
2 Make a list of all the different motives suggested by the sources and information on these pages.
3 Which of the Crusaders shown in the pictures might say each of these things and how would they finish their sentence?
   I was inspired to go on Crusade by …
   I hope that going on Crusade …
   Going on Crusade is better than …
4 Write a web page to give a better answer to the question 'Who were the Crusaders?'
   Think about:
   ● Were they all soldiers?
   ● Were they all fighting for religious reasons?

Knights

SOURCE 9 *Some of the rights of Crusaders listed by the Pope in 1215*

● The property and family of Crusaders were protected while they were away.
● Crusaders paid no taxes while they were on Crusade.
● Crusaders' debts need not be paid until they returned.

Monk-knights

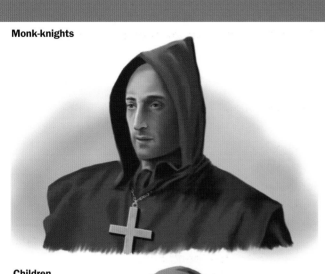

Children

Common soldiers

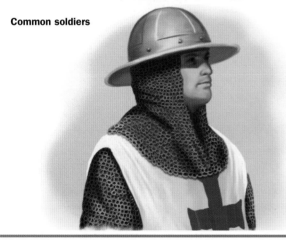

The leaders became famous but tens of thousands of ordinary people fought on both sides in the Crusades. One source tells the story of a Christian woman who was carrying soil to build an earthwork during a siege when she was wounded by a spear. Before she died, she begged her husband to use her body as part of the defences to help stop their enemies' attack.

SOURCE 10 *The Christian leader St Bernard of Clairvaux said these words to encourage the Knights of the Temple, who were monk-knights. They lived like monks, praying several times a day, but were also ferocious soldiers, dedicated to winning back Jerusalem*

Go forward and drive off the enemies of Christ. Rejoice if you live and conquer but rejoice and glory more if you die and go to the Lord.

SOURCE 11 *A German chronicler describes the beginning of the Children's Crusade in 1212. Nicholas was a twelve-year-old boy. He had a dream that God told him to lead children to capture the city of Jerusalem. God told him that this Crusade, unlike all the previous ones, would succeed. He preached about his vision all over Cologne and persuaded people to join him*

Boys and girls, and some men and women, set out with Nicholas, all penniless. Nobody could stop them, neither their parents nor their friends. People did anything to join the expedition.

SOURCE 12 *Many people in Europe lived in extreme poverty. Chrétien de Troyes, a twelfth-century poet, describes the attitudes of young workers at the time*

Forever will we weave silk,
But never will we be well dressed,
Forever we'll be poor and naked,
Forever will we hunger and thirst
But the man we toil for
Gets rich because of us.

ACTIVITY 2

Discuss

5 Think about why people today might join an army or join in a war. Are their reasons similar to or different from those of the Crusaders?

6 Why would studying the Crusades be dangerous if you ignored the fact that people had different motives for fighting?

What were relationships like between Christians and Muslims in the Middle Ages?

SOURCE 13 *1095 – Pope Urban's speech persuading Christians to go on the First Crusade*

Our Christian brothers who live in the East urgently need your help. The Arabs [Muslims] have attacked them and have taken over Christian land. They have killed and captured many people and destroyed the churches. The Lord God appeals to you ... soldiers and knights, rich and poor, to sweep our enemies from the lands of our Christian friends.

SOURCE 14 *A German chronicler describes what happened in Germany in 1096*

The Crusaders slaughtered many Jews in Germany, claiming that this was the beginning of their Crusade because they were killing enemies of Christianity.

Events like these happened in England at the time of the third Crusade in the 1180s. Many Jews were murdered in York, Norwich and Stamford.

SOURCE 15 *From a chronicle written by a soldier who went on the First Crusade. He is describing the capture of Jerusalem in 1099. The Crusaders had taken many months to travel from Europe*

Before we attacked Jerusalem, the bishops ordered everyone to walk around the walls of the city and pray as they walked. At dawn we attacked the city from all sides ... One of our knights, called Lethold, climbed over the city wall. All the city's defenders fled from the wall. Our men followed, killing and beheading the defenders all the way. There was such a slaughter for a whole day but, finally, they were beaten. Our men captured men and women. They killed them or let them live as they saw fit. Soon our men were running all around the city, seizing gold and silver, horses and mules and houses filled with all kinds of goods.

SOURCE 16 *Fulcher of Chartres (1059–1127) wrote a detailed history of the Crusaders. He joined the First Crusade in 1096 and lived in Jerusalem until he died*

We used to be Europeans, now we are Easterners. The men who were from Rome or France have become Galileans or Palestinians. We have already forgotten the places where we were born. Some have married women from this land, either Christians or Moslems [Muslims] who have been baptised.

SOURCE 17 *Ibn Jubayr (1144–1217) was a Muslim trader from Spain who travelled through the Middle East in the 1180s*

We travelled through many farms and villages whose lands are well farmed. The people are all Moslems but they live in comfort with the Europeans. Their houses belong to them and their property is unharmed. All the land, villages and farms stayed in the hands of the Moslems ...The two sides understand each other completely. The men of war fight their war but the people stay at peace.

SOURCE 18 *An extract from the autobiography of Usamah Ibn Munqidh (1095–1188). Usamah was a Muslim nobleman who knew all the Muslim leaders and many Christian leaders*

The Franks [Europeans] who have come recently are always more inhuman than the Franks who have lived among us and are used to Muslims.

A proof of the harshness of the Franks (the scourge of Allah upon them) can be seen in what happened to me when I visited Jerusalem. I went into the mosque Al-Aqsa. By the side was a little mosque that the Franks had made into a church. The Christian Templars were in charge of the mosques. They were my friends and let me say my prayers in the little mosque. I was praying when a Frank rushed at me, seized me and turned my face to the east saying 'That is how to pray'. A group of Templars took hold of him and threw him out. I returned to my prayers. The same Frank came back and forced my face round to the east, repeating 'That is how to pray'. The Templars again threw him out and they apologised to me. 'He is a stranger who has only just arrived. He has never seen anyone praying without turning to the east.' I went out and saw how he was trembling with shock after seeing me pray towards Mecca.

ACTIVITY 2

Discuss

5 Why would studying the Crusades be dangerous if you only included descriptions of massacres and cruelty?

SOURCE 19 *Roger Bacon, an English churchman and scientist, writing in 1260*

War is not effective because those who survive, together with their children, are more and more embittered against their enemies.

Richard or Saladin: who was the hero?

ACTIVITY 1

Here's the answer many people would give to the question above:

Richard the Lionheart was the greatest hero of the Crusades.

1 Examine the sources on these two pages. Look carefully at the information about the writers. Then write a web page to give a better answer to the question.

> **i** The city of Acre had surrendered to King Richard after an 18-month siege. Richard held thousands of prisoners, expecting ransom payments from Saladin, the Muslim leader.

Richard the Lionheart

▲ **SOURCE 20** *Richard I was King of England 1189–1199 although his favourite lands were in France. He spoke little English and spent little time in England. But he is regarded as a great English hero. This statue is outside the Houses of Parliament. Richard twice led his army towards Jerusalem in 1192 but decided not to attack. He knew that his army was not strong enough to hold the city for long. Finally he agreed a truce with Saladin and sailed home.*

SOURCE 21 *Taken from* The Journey of King Richard *by an English churchman*

King Richard, alone, berserk, came on the Muslims. No man could escape his sword. He made a clear path as if mowing hay with a scythe.

... Richard waited three weeks for Saladin to release the Christian prisoners and return the Holy Cross. But Saladin only sent gifts and messages and did not keep his promises. A council of the Crusaders' leaders agreed to behead the Muslim prisoners. King Richard ordered that 2,700 prisoners be led out of the city and be executed.

1 What do these two writers agree about?
2 What do they disagree about?

SOURCE 22 *Written by Baha ad-Din, Saladin's secretary*

This King of England was courageous, energetic and daring in combat. When he arrived at Acre the Franks let out cries of joy. The Muslims were filled with fear.

... The English king broke his word to the Muslim prisoners who had surrendered the city in return for their lives. If Saladin paid their ransom they were to be freed. If he did not they were to become slaves. When he saw that Saladin delayed payment he secretly changed his mind. Even after he received the money he ordered the cold-blooded slaughter of more than 3,000 men.

ACTIVITY 2

Discuss:

2 Why would studying the Crusades be dangerous if you only studied Richard or Saladin instead of finding out about both?

Saladin the Great

Saladin re-conquered large areas of the Crusader kingdom. His greatest victory was the Battle of Hattin in July 1187. Among the prisoners were King Guy of Jerusalem and Reynold of Châtillon.

After the battle, Saladin gave the King iced water to drink. The King drank and gave the rest to Reynold but Saladin said 'This godless man did not have my permission to drink and will not save his life that way'. Then, with his own hand, he cut off Reynold's head. 'Twice,' said Saladin, 'I have sworn to kill that man. Once when he attacked Mecca and Medina, and again when he broke the truce and attacked the traders.' Saladin also ordered the execution of all the Knights Templar and Knights Hospitaller, the soldier-monks.

A few months later Saladin re-captured Jerusalem. The Muslims took Christian crosses down from the mosques but there was no other looting or destruction in the city. There was no revenge for the way the Crusaders had treated the Muslim holy places in 1099. Rich prisoners were set free after paying ransoms. Some of the poor were set free without a ransom but many others were made slaves. Christians were not forced to leave Jerusalem. The native people who were Christians were allowed to stay and worship in the churches. Saladin also invited Jews to return to Jerusalem.

▼ **SOURCE 23** *This is the only Muslim picture of Saladin. There are few descriptions but he was surprisingly short and frail. His full name was Salah ad-Din Yusuf Ibn Ayyub. He died in 1193.*

SOURCE 24 *From a biography of Saladin by Baha ad-Din who was a member of Saladin's household 1188–1193*

Once, when I was riding at Saladin's side, an army scout came to us with a sobbing woman.

She said, 'Yesterday some Muslim thieves entered my tent and stole my little girl. I cried all night and our commanders told me that Saladin is merciful, go to him and ask for your daughter back. I place all my hopes in you.'

Saladin was touched and tears came to his eyes. He sent someone to the slave market to look for the girl, and later a horseman arrived bearing the child on his shoulders. All those present wept. Thus was her daughter returned to her.

SOURCE 25 *Written by William of Tyre, a Christian Archbishop who lived most of his life in the Holy Land and knew Saladin*

Saladin was a wise man, valiant in war and generous beyond all measure.

THE BIG STORY: Conflict Part One

You've found out a lot about war in the Middle Ages. Now it's time to sum up your Big Story of conflict in the Middle Ages in one mind map! Here is our summary of this Big Story but it is missing examples and evidence and a couple of strands are completely empty. Your task is either to create your own mind map from scratch or add examples to ours to make it your own.

HOW TO...

... make a Big Story mind map

1 Use a large piece of plain paper and lots of coloured pencils or pens.
2 In the middle write your topic – what this mind map is about.
3 Draw a branch showing your first big question. Use a different colour for every branch.
4 Subdivide the branch into twigs – one for each answer to that question. Add evidence or examples and a drawing.
5 Carry on adding branches and twigs – as many times as you want.

KEY POINTS
· Use a different colour for each branch
· Add drawings that sum up the details
· Use single words and phrases not long sentences

LEARNING LOG

Use your mind map to record the key points about war in the Middle Ages so you will remember them next year.

Peer review
Now join up with another person and compare your mind maps.
a) Name at least one thing you like about the other map.
b) Think of one way to improve each map.
c) Why is it important to share ideas and learn from each other?

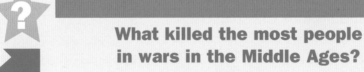

What killed the most people in wars in the Middle Ages?

The answer is – dirty water! Soldiers caught illnesses like dysentery (extreme diarrhoea) from drinking dirty water. More Normans died in 1066 from dysentery while camped in England than died at the Battle of Hastings. Men died during sieges of castles and towns because diseases spread rapidly through camps. Even the great Henry V (pages 86–87) died of dysentery.

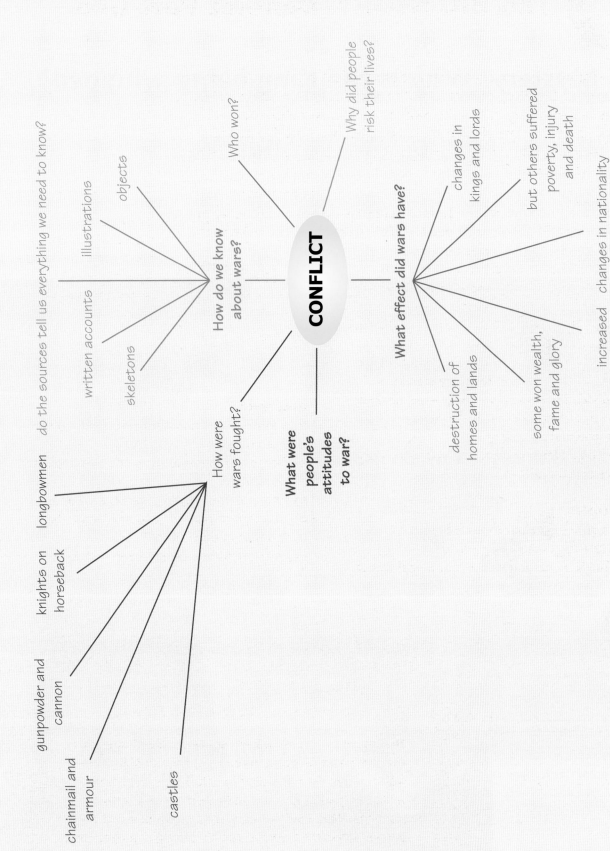

CONFLICT

How do we know about wars?
- do the sources tell us everything we need to know?
- illustrations
- objects
- written accounts
- skeletons

Who won?

Why did people risk their lives?

What effect did wars have?
- changes in kings and lords
- but others suffered poverty, injury and death
- changes in nationality and language
- increased hatred
- some won wealth, fame and glory
- destruction of homes and lands

How were wars fought?
- longbowmen
- knights on horseback
- gunpowder and cannon
- chainmail and armour
- castles

What were people's attitudes to war?

Mystery: Why is the King being whipped?

One Friday in July 1174, King Henry II walked three miles barefoot, dressed only in a rough woollen tunic, to Canterbury Cathedral. At the cathedral Henry was greeted by a silent line of bishops, abbots and monks. Henry lay face down on the stone floor of the cathedral and prayed, then he knelt by the tomb of Thomas Becket and, one by one, the bishops and abbots whipped the King five times. Then it was the turn of the 80 monks. Each monk whipped the King three times.

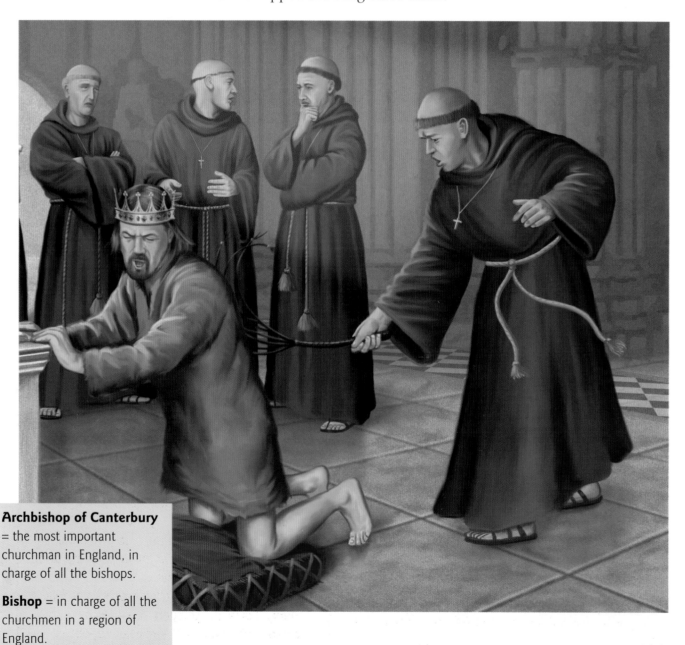

Archbishop of Canterbury = the most important churchman in England, in charge of all the bishops.

Bishop = in charge of all the churchmen in a region of England.

CLUE 1

Henry made Thomas Becket Archbishop of Canterbury in 1162. Henry thought his friend would help him to take control of the bishops. Instead, Becket sided with the bishops and the two men quarrelled.

Becket lived in France from 1164 until 1169 to escape from the quarrel.

CLUE 3

Two days after Henry was whipped, his army captured the King of Scotland. Then he beat the rest of the rebels. Many people said that God gave him the victory because he had shown how sorry he was for Becket's death.

CLUE 5

Henry asked the Pope for support against the rebels. The Pope said that he and God would support Henry if Henry showed how sorry he was for Becket's murder. He said Henry must let himself be punished and give land and money to the Church.

CLUE 8 *This account of the murder of Thomas Becket, Archbishop of Canterbury, on 29 December 1170, was written by Edward Grim, a monk who saw Becket murdered*

The murderers came in full armour, carrying swords and axes. The monks shouted to the Archbishop to escape but the Archbishop refused.

In a mad fury, the knights called out, 'Where is Thomas Becket, traitor to the King and to the country?' The Archbishop, quite unafraid, answered, 'Here I am, no traitor to the King but a priest.'

'You shall die this instant,' they cried. They pulled and dragged him, trying to get him outside the cathedral, but they could not do so. Then a knight leapt at him and wounded him in the head. Another knight struck him on the head, but still he stood.

At the third blow he fell to his knees, saying in a low voice, 'For the name of Jesus I am about to die.'

The next blow cut off the top of his head and blood white with brain and the brain red with blood stained the floor.

CLUE 2

There was a great rebellion against Henry in 1173 and 1174. His own wife and sons allied with the Kings of France and Scotland and fought against Henry. He was in danger of losing many of his lands.

CLUE 4

Thomas Becket was Henry's friend and main adviser for many years during the 1150s and early 1160s.

CLUE 6

In the 1150s Henry quarrelled with the bishops about who was in charge of the churchmen in England. Henry said he should choose the bishops but the bishops said that was the job of the Pope.

CLUE 7

In December 1170 Becket returned to England. He was met by cheering crowds. When Henry heard this, he lost his temper and shouted, 'Are all my men traitors and cowards? Why do you let this low-born priest treat me with such contempt?' Four of his knights set off for Canterbury.

ACTIVITY

Work with a partner, use the clues and see if you can work out the mystery of why Henry II was being whipped by the monks.

Tips

a) You could draw a timeline of events from 1154–1174. Not all the clues have dates but you can work out a sequence for those that don't.

b) Look for links between the clues. Some of them are connected and this is an important part of solving the mystery.

c) At the end, write a paragraph explaining why Henry II is being whipped. Make sure you explain *why*, don't just say what happened.

What was a medieval king supposed to do?

Would you have liked to be a medieval king? Find out what a king did with the help of this day in the life of a Superking!

1 Look good!

"It is important to look rich and powerful."

Get up early, dress in fine, colourful clothes while servants bring food.

2

"I am God's representative so I must pray and worship him."

Go to chapel for prayers. I must show my support for the bishops and the Church.

ACTIVITY 1

1 Write a heading for each picture to sum up what a good king had to do. We have done picture 1 for you.
2 Which of these jobs do you think was:
   a) the trickiest
   b) the easiest
   c) the most important?
Keep a note of your ideas. You will return to this question later.

ACTIVITY 2

3 Government has changed since the Middle Ages. Copy and complete this table to show who does each of the King's jobs today.

	Prime Minister	Monarch
Who decides about going to war?		
Who decides when Parliament starts and finishes?		
Who decides how much tax is collected?		
Who decides how to punish crimes?		
Who goes to ceremonies and wears the grandest clothing?		

3

> I think it is time to invade France. Do you agree?

Meet my advisers. They are mostly nobles and churchmen who own lots of land. It is important to listen to their advice. That makes them feel trusted and they trust me, but in the end I always take the decisions. My most important decisions are about war because it is my duty to defend my lands and people against enemies.

4

> Sort out your quarrel by the time I finish dinner, or you will both be executed.

Hear the case of Balkwill versus Awklord. These two knights have been arguing about land. One attacked the other's castle. I give them a choice. Sort out your quarrel by the time I finish dinner, or you will both be executed. A king has to keep law and order. It is one of my most important tasks.

5

> I need money to pay for the war so I shall ask Parliament to collect a new tax.

I have a few hours to go hunting or I might practise my fighting skills with my sword and lance. For dinner, I change into even grander clothes and some fine jewellery. The Archbishop of Canterbury is my dinner guest. I tell him I will be calling a Parliament to give me taxes for my war.

6

> Now you are fifteen you are nearly old enough to govern the country if I die. But I hope that will not be for a long time yet!

After dinner I'll visit my Queen and our new baby son. She has borne me four fine sons – all that a king could want. She's a good wife to have produced so many heirs.

103

Into the mind of a medieval king!

Power!

In this section the Big Story is about power – about who ruled England and what they did. We are starting with kings, because in the Middle Ages they had most power. But even then there were limits….

The barons

The barons (also called nobles) were the rich families who owned lots of land. They were mostly descended from the Normans who had been given land by William the Conqueror. They provided an army for the King when he needed it and kept order in their own areas of England. So the King had to keep them happy. The barons had rebelled against the King before. They might do so again.

They usually wanted the King to do things that made them richer. They were not very interested in helping ordinary people.

The Church

Religion helped the King because people believed he had been chosen by God. Therefore anyone who fought against him was fighting against God. People did not believe that was a good thing to do because if they disobeyed God they might not get to heaven.

However, what happened if the King quarrelled with the bishops and archbishops? Then they might say that God was angry with the King and people should fight against him. So the King had to keep the churchmen happy as well.

The King in the middle

So although the King was powerful he had to keep the support of these two groups. An example of how the barons and the Church could limit a king's power was the mystery you on page 100–101. The reason Henry agreed to be whipped in 1174 was that he faced a serious rebellion. To win back the support of the barons and the bishops, he had to apologise for Becket's death and accept some punishment.

ACTIVITY

1 Look at the 'power line' below. Where on the line do you think King Henry II stood?

2 Do you think kings will move more to the left, more to the right or stay in the same place through the Middle Ages?

3 Do you think that barons would be eager or reluctant to rebel against a king?

4 The king is thinking about how to rule England. Write his thought bubbles, using pages 100–103 to help you. Keep them. At the end of the section you will come back to these bubbles again.

0	1	2	3	4	5	6	7	8	9	10

POWER

The King has to do what his barons tell him

The King can do what he likes

My most important tasks as king are...

My biggest fear is...

People think I can do whatever I like but...

My barons will obey me if...

Why did the barons rebel against King John?

Now you know what a 'Superking' was supposed to do it is time to investigate a king who wasn't super at all, King John. Your task is to work out what went wrong for John and why the barons rebelled against him.

Your enquiry – stage 1: Why were the barons angry with King John?

ACTIVITY 1

This scorecard shows how we think the barons would have scored King John.

1 Read the story strip on pages 107–109 and fill in the last column with evidence about John's successes and failures in each category.
2 Decide whether you agree with us about how the barons would score King John. Change any that you think are too high or too low.
3 Which three jobs in column 1 do you think mattered most to the barons? Explain why you chose them.

What should a king do?	Score out of 10 (as awarded by the barons)	Evidence for the barons' score
1. Look rich and powerful to impress your people	8	
2. Win the support and trust of the barons and listen to their advice	1	
3. Lead the army, win wars and keep your land	0	
4. Raise taxes fairly, in the same ways as kings before you	0	
5. Stamp out crime and keep order in the country	5	
6. Support the Church	2	
7. Have sons so there are no disputes over who is the next king	7	
Overall judgement	2	

Timecheck

Here are the events of 1066–1216 so you can see where King John's reign fits in with events you have already studied.

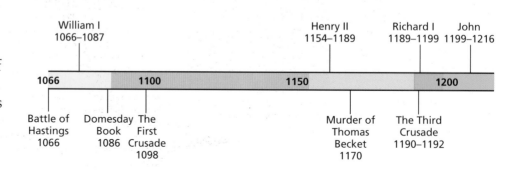

The career of King John

1 A successful father

John was born in 1167, the youngest son of King Henry II. Henry raised high taxes to pay for wars to defend his empire, which included half of France (see map). Henry was such a good soldier the barons paid up. He also quarrelled with the Church. He said he should choose the archbishops.

2 Lackland

Henry gave his eldest sons lots of land but had none left to give John, so John was nicknamed 'Lackland'. Then Henry sent nineteen-year-old John to rule Ireland. He upset the Irish barons by giggling at their long beards. They rebelled. John returned to England. He had failed to gain any land.

3 A successful brother

John's brother Richard was crowned king in 1189. Richard was an even greater soldier than Henry. He spent most of his reign on Crusade. He increased taxes to pay for his wars. While he was away, John plotted with King Philip of France to conquer some of Richard's land. But when Richard came home John didn't dare fight him.

4 A rival for the throne

John became king in 1199. However, he had a rival. Some of the barons in France wanted John's twelve-year-old nephew, Arthur of Brittany, to be king. In 1202, John captured Arthur. Many people believed that John had Arthur murdered. Others said that John killed Arthur in a drunken rage and threw him in the River Seine.

5 Soft-sword

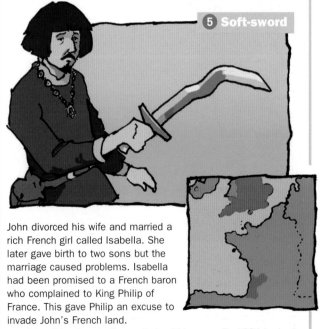

John divorced his wife and married a rich French girl called Isabella. She later gave birth to two sons but the marriage caused problems. Isabella had been promised to a French baron who complained to King Philip of France. This gave Philip an excuse to invade John's French land.

John did not go to France to lead his army. By 1204 he had lost nearly all his land in France (see map) and had got a new nickname: 'Soft-sword.'

6 John quarrels with the barons

John was desperate to win back his lands in France. He asked the barons to provide an army, just as they had for his father and brother. Some refused. They did not trust John. They did not like the way he took important decisions without consulting them. They did not see why they should spend money and risk their lives when their lands were in England, not France.

7 Raising money

Without the soldiers provided by the barons John had to raise money to pay for an army. To do this, he:

- increased the fines people had to pay in the courts
- charged rich widows as much as £3000 for the right to stay unmarried after their husbands died
- increased the tax people paid to the King when they inherited their parents' land. He charged one baron £6000 for land that was only earning £550 per year
- massively increased taxes on barons who refused to provide soldiers for him
- when one baron did not pay, he imprisoned him without trial until he paid.

By 1213 he had collected so much tax that almost half of all the coins in England were stored in his castles, ready to pay for a new war. This made him very unpopular.

8 John the judge

John worked hard as king in England. He was very interested in the law. He sat as a judge in the Royal Court and decided cases himself. But people said he was biased and he used the courts to help his friends and punish people he did not like. He also travelled around the country checking that the barons were keeping the laws. The barons resented John's involvement. After all, Henry and Richard had spent most of their time abroad. But John didn't have any choice as he'd lost most of his empire.

9 Who were his friends?

John did not trust the English barons. He preferred to listen to the advice of foreign mercenaries (men who were paid to fight for him) like Gerard d'Athee. John put Gerard in charge of three major castles in Gloucester, Bristol and Hereford after taking them from English barons.

⑩ Looking good

According to royal records the King had a bath once every three weeks. Each bath cost 6d, which means it was quite an elaborate ceremony – compare this with monks who were expected to bathe just three times a year! King John was also famously well dressed. He particularly liked exotic fur coats made of sable, ermine and even polar bear. When he was young he had thick, curly hair, but later he became bald and fat.

⑪ John quarrels with the Pope

The Pope punished John by passing an interdict over John's lands. This meant that church services stopped. No marriages or burials could take place.

In 1205 John quarrelled with the Pope, just as his father had done. They disagreed over who should be the new Archbishop of Canterbury. John refused to let the Pope's choice, Stephen Langton, enter the country. It had always been the King's right to choose the Archbishop and the barons agreed with him over this.

John retaliated by taking away all the Church's property.

In 1209, the Pope excommunicated John. This meant that John would go to hell when he died. Next the Archbishop threatened to excommunicate all of John's soldiers. In 1213, John gave in to the Pope.

⑫ Disaster in France

And finally, there was John's biggest problem: his empire. He was determined to reclaim the land he had lost in France. In 1214, John and the Emperor of Germany agreed to attack France. But once again John did not ask his barons for their advice, and did not get their support. Many refused to fight, but John went ahead anyway. He raised an army of mercenaries and invaded the south of France.

He left the German Emperor to fight the King of France. It was his biggest gamble, and he lost. The Emperor was beaten by the French at the Battle of Bouvines. John's hopes of regaining his land in France were over. All those taxes had been wasted.

Your enquiry – stage 2: How did the barons try to solve the problem?

Now you know why the barons gave John such a bad scorecard. After his defeat in France in 1214 they saw their chance. They did not want to get rid of him as king but they did want him to change the way he was ruling England. What happened next was one of the most famous events in English history.

Solution 1: Magna Carta

In January 1215 the barons met the King. They demanded he must change the way he ruled the country. John agreed to a meeting in April, but did not turn up!

It looked as though a civil war was going to start between John and the rebel barons, but there were also many barons who did not want civil war, including the great William Marshal (see page 50). They talked both sides into attending a meeting at Runnymede, near Windsor Castle, in June.

John agreed to some rules about how to govern the country. These rules were written down in a charter, known as Magna Carta – The Great Charter.

Magna Carta contained 63 rules (called Clauses) describing how the King should treat all freemen in the country. The freemen were the barons, bishops and merchants. Magna Carta did not say anything about ordinary people.

ACTIVITY 1

1 Here are seven of the most important clauses from Magna Carta, but they are incomplete.

If you had been one of the barons how would you have finished off each of these clauses? Use pages 107–109 to help you. Your teacher will be able to tell you what the actual document said.

2 Discuss with a partner why you think John especially disliked Clause 61.

3 One of these clauses is still very important today. Which one do you think this is?

Clause 1. The English Church shall be ... The King must not ... with the Church.

Clause 2. When a baron inherits land he shall not ...

Clause 8. No widow shall be forced to ... as long as she wishes to live without a ...

Clause 12. The King must not demand taxes without ...

Clause 39. No freeman shall be arrested or imprisoned without ...

Clause 51. All ... soldiers must leave the country.

Clause 61. The barons shall choose 25 barons to make certain the King keeps this charter. If he breaks the charter, the 25 barons can take action to make him keep it. They can take his castles and lands but must not attack the King, his Queen or his children.

Solution 2: Rebellion!

13 John breaks the charter

John never intended to keep to the rules of Magna Carta. He objected to Clause 61 in particular because he believed that nobody could tell the King what to do. He had only agreed to Magna Carta to win time to build up an army to fight the barons. He was determined to beat them. He even got the Pope's support after telling him that he had been *forced* to sign Magna Carta.

14 Civil war

The rebel barons decided that it was time to have a new king. They invited Prince Louis of France to take over as king and captured London but John captured Rochester Castle. That was when he used the fat pigs (see page 82) as his secret weapon.

15 Destruction

The civil war went on for months. John led his army on a long march through his enemies' lands, burning and destroying whatever he could. It was like the Harrying of the North after the Norman Conquest. Neither side risked fighting a battle in case they lost, but gradually the rebels captured more and more of John's castles.

16 John dies

While taking a shortcut, John lost some of the Crown jewels when his baggage train sank in the quicksand of The Wash. Shortly afterwards, John died from dysentery (fever with serious diarrhoea) after eating too many peaches and drinking too much beer!

17 King Henry

Now John was dead, the civil war ended. The barons decided that there was more chance of peace if John's son, nine-year-old Henry, became king.

ACTIVITY 2

Discuss:

4 Why did Magna Carta not solve the problems between John and his barons?

5 Why do you think the barons fought a civil war with John in 1216, not 1214, before Magna Carta?

DOING HISTORY:
Causes and consequences

Your enquiry – stage 3:
Thinking about causes

You are investigating why the barons rebelled against King John in 1216.

> **Causes**
>
> Most events have a number of causes

Important events nearly always have a range of causes. There are seven cause cards below, but even that is not the whole story.

1. The cards show seven different causes. In pairs take one each and explain **how** it helped cause the rebellion. For example:
   B. John murdering his nephew Arthur helped cause the rebellion because it made the barons distrust John from the start.

2. From your knowledge of John and the barons, add at least one more cause card.

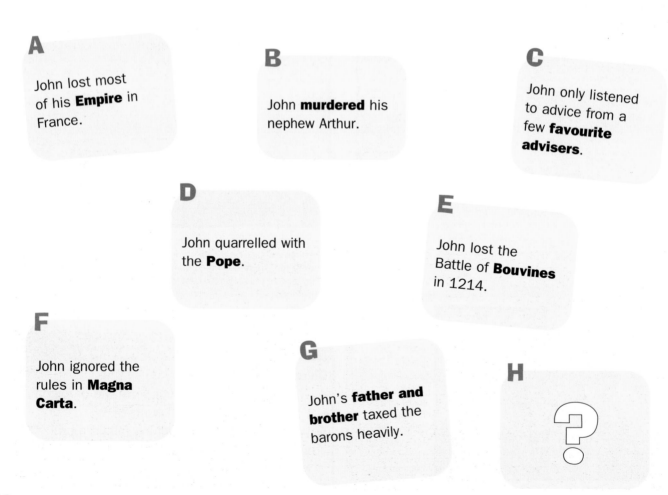

A John lost most of his **Empire** in France.

B John **murdered** his nephew Arthur.

C John only listened to advice from a few **favourite advisers**.

D John quarrelled with the **Pope**.

E John lost the Battle of **Bouvines** in 1214.

F John ignored the rules in **Magna Carta**.

G John's **father and brother** taxed the barons heavily.

H ?

Causes

Even if there are lots of causes there's still usually one that finally sets off an event – the trigger

③ Which of the cards shows the event that triggered the rebellion in 1216?

Causes

Causes are not equally important

You will do more work on causes later in this course. How will you record these big ideas so you can remember them and use them next time?

④ Arrange the cause cards to make a pattern explaining why the barons rebelled against John in 1216. Put what you think is the most important cause at the top of your diagram, the least important at the bottom. You could copy one of the patterns below or make a pattern of your own.

⑤ Which pattern – 1 or 2 – does each of the pictures below fit?

Pattern 1

This pattern is good if you think one cause is more important than all the other causes.

Pattern 2

This pattern is good if you think that two causes were equally important and the rest were less important but equal.

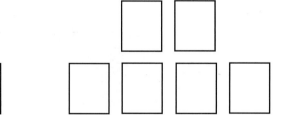

Your enquiry – stage 4: Writing about causes

Your final task will be to write a short essay **Why did the barons rebel against King John in 1216?** This is asking you to explain the causes of the rebellion. You have already done the hardest part – thinking about the causes – all that you have to do now is turn that thinking into some writing. But we are going to help you….

- A good paragraph starts with **an opening statement** that summarises the **argument** of the paragraph and links the paragraph to the question.
- The opening statement is followed by **evidence**. It is very important that you provide evidence to support your **argument**. Why should people believe your argument if you do not have any evidence to back it up? The more evidence you use the stronger your argument becomes.
- It finishes with a **concluding statement**. This statement gives your **answer** to the **question** you have been asked and it links the evidence to the question. If you include evidence but do not use a concluding statement to link the evidence to the question then the evidence is pointless.

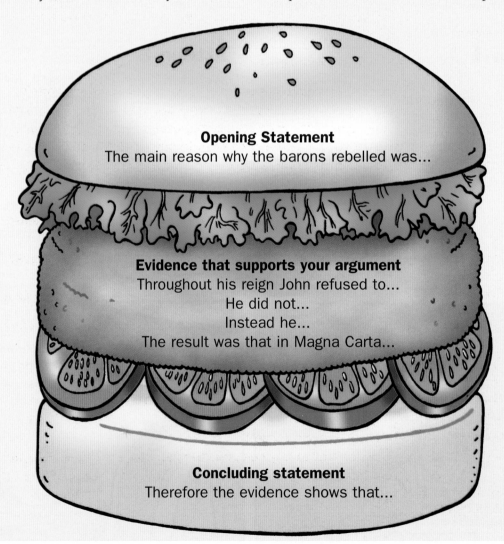

Opening Statement
The main reason why the barons rebelled was…

Evidence that supports your argument
Throughout his reign John refused to…
He did not…
Instead he…
The result was that in Magna Carta…

Concluding statement
Therefore the evidence shows that…

Now try writing your own hamburger paragraph, which will be part of your essay **Why did the barons rebel against King John in 1216?** Choose whichever of these three options best suits you.

Option 1 – check our paragraph
a) Here is a paragraph that someone else has written. Check it against the hamburger guidance. On your own copy underline in different colours:
- the opening statement
- the supporting evidence
- the concluding statement.

One of the big disagreements between John and the barons was taxes. John increased the taxes paid by the barons in order to pay for his wars. He collected so many taxes that half of all the coins in England were in his treasury. In Magna Carta the barons made John reduce taxes such as the tax when a baron inherited land so that proves taxes must have been a big issue for the barons. So the evidence suggests that John's taxes were a cause of the rebellion.

b) Discuss: how could you improve this paragraph?

Option 2 – use the ingredients to write your own paragraph
Here are the ingredients for a paragraph about John's 'advisers'. Use these ingredients to construct your own hamburger paragraph.
a) Choose one of the sentences to put in the top bun of the hamburger.
b) Choose two more sentences as your evidence, and provide details from the story to support it.
c) Now decide what goes in the bottom bun. You could use our sentence starter or write your own. It is up to you. Write a short sentence to sum up the main point of the paragraph.
d) Re-read your paragraph. Do you want to make any changes?

For example when the barons refused to provide an army for John he…

One very important reason the barons rebelled against King John was because he did not ask their advice.

The evidence suggests that John seemed to think he could…

To make matters worse he did ask advice from…

Option 3 – do it yourself
If you don't need any help, use the hamburger approach to write a paragraph about one of the causes you put in the top of your diagram on page 113.

HOW TO…

… write a good paragraph

A good paragraph is like a good hamburger. The opening and concluding statements are the buns which hold the burger together. The evidence is the meat which comes between the buns. Just as all parts of a hamburger are important for a balanced meal, all parts of the paragraph are important too.

- If you forget the meat (the evidence) or there is not much of it, the meal is tasteless.
- If you forget the bottom bun (the concluding statement) the meat/evidence falls out.

How to write a good essay

A good essay has a strong sense of direction and a clear argument. It is also written in clear paragraphs which are packed full of evidence to make it really strong.

READY FOR ACTION!

1 **A clear introduction!**

The introduction announces your arrival and gets you moving in the right direction. It impresses your reader that you know what you are doing. For example:

In this essay I will explain why I think the barons rebelled against King John in 1216. Some of the causes go right back to the beginning of John's reign and had been building up for years, but there were other causes which actually triggered the rebellion. I will investigate both and explain why I think that (...you insert) was the most important cause of the rebellion.

2 **What was a king expected to do?**

This can be based on the work you did on pages 102–105. Don't just list all the jobs – instead focus on the jobs that you think were the most important and why these were so important.

3 **Long-term causes: Why were the barons dissatisfied with John?**

This is the main part of the essay. These paragraphs explain the causes that built up over time as the barons became more and more dissatisfied with how John was running the country. You have much more evidence from pages 106–113 than you can fit in one essay so you need to select just the causes that you think are most important in making the barons dissatisfied with the King. The diagram you made on page 113 will help you.

Write as many paragraphs as you need, but make sure each one makes a new point. You could write paragraphs about:
● taxes
● wars and loss of lords
● advisers and trust
● the Church.
You can recycle your practice hamburger paragraphs from the previous page.
And remember the hamburger advice.

116

4 **An option – John's defence**

John did not get everything wrong and he inherited problems from his father and brother, so you could write a paragraph defending King John.

5 **Short-term causes: What finally triggered the rebellion?**

All these problems might have made a rebellion possible or even likely but it was Magna Carta and John's response to it that finally led to rebellion and civil war.

So this paragraph explains how and why that happened. How did tension and mistrust turn into outright rebellion?

6 **Conclusion**

An essay needs a conclusion.
- Recap the most important reason for the rebellion.
- Recap your most important piece of evidence to support it.

Think about this: if you did not put a trigger event at the top of your diagram on page 113 and yet this was what actually caused the rebellion, what does this tell you about causes?

JOB DONE!

7 **Check your work**

Do not miss out this stage. Check your essay carefully.
- Do you think the writing is interesting?
- Have you made your viewpoint clear?
- Have you supported it with evidence?
- Is it neatly presented, and is the spelling and punctuation accurate?

The Rebellion Steps: how high did they climb?

In 1216 the barons were not trying to get rid of King John. They simply wanted to make him agree some rules for how he governed the country. Later in the Middle Ages there were more rebellions against kings who did not accept these rules. Find out about how far up the Rebellion Steps the barons went. Did they ever try to get rid of kings completely?

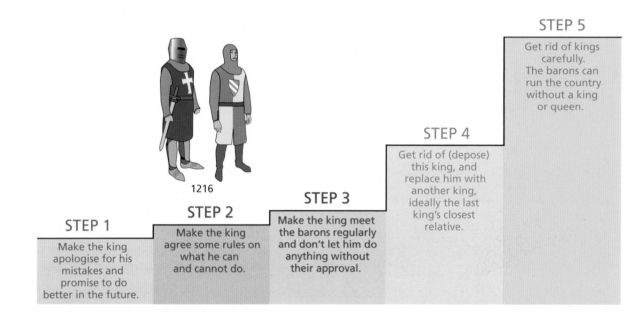

STEP 5
Get rid of kings carefully. The barons can run the country without a king or queen.

STEP 4
Get rid of (depose) this king, and replace him with another king, ideally the last king's closest relative.

STEP 3
Make the king meet the barons regularly and don't let him do anything without their approval.

STEP 2
Make the king agree some rules on what he can and cannot do.

STEP 1
Make the king apologise for his mistakes and promise to do better in the future.

1216

ACTIVITY

1 a) Draw your own version of these Rebellion Steps.

b) Take each rebellion opposite and decide which step the rebels reached. We have already shown where 1216 belongs.

c) Write the date of each rebellion on the correct step.

2 Look at the completed steps. What is the difference between what happened in the two rebellions in the 1200s and what happened in the two rebellions in the 1300s?

3 Most barons would have agreed with the statements below in 1216. From the evidence on page 119 which would they still agree with in the 1300s?

> **a)** Kings are chosen by God. We can't get rid of a king who has been chosen by God.

> **b)** To fight a war you need a king who is a good soldier and can organise and lead the army.

> **c)** I can't imagine a country without a king. Unthinkable!

4 Why do you think the barons never reached Step 5?

A 1258 HENRY III

Henry was King John's son. He became king when he was only nine. He agreed to follow the rules in Magna Carta. But when Henry grew up it was a different story. He did things like relying on French advisers and becoming involved in an expensive war in Sicily. Then he lent the Pope a huge amount of money for a war – without discussing this with the barons. Simon de Montfort and other barons forced Henry to hold regular meetings (called Parliaments) to make sure he governed the country according to the rules in Magna Carta but they did not try to replace him as king.

B 1327 EDWARD II

Edward II was a poor soldier who lost wars against the Scots but that did not cause a rebellion. What made the barons angry was that Edward listened to the advice of his friend, Piers Gaveston, and ignored them. In 1311 the barons forced Edward to send Gaveston abroad. He came back but was caught and executed by the Duke of Lancaster. Edward hated Lancaster for that and ten years later had his revenge – he had Lancaster taken prisoner and beheaded without trial. Lancaster had simply been murdered on the King's orders. This led to civil war. The barons took Edward prisoner and made his son king instead. Soon afterwards Edward was murdered at Berkeley Castle, Gloucestershire, probably on the orders of his wife, Isabella, and Roger Mortimer.

C 1399 RICHARD II

Richard became king in 1377 when he was ten. Four years later he was a hero when he faced thousands of rebels in London and persuaded them to go home (see pages 180–181). Maybe this made Richard think he could do anything he wanted to do. He made two mistakes. Firstly he gave money and land away to his favourite advisers. Secondly, he made peace with France when the barons thought he should be fighting to win more land there. They rebelled in 1386 and took over running the country. Richard was furious but he had to wait to take his revenge. Ten years later he had his enemies executed or forced to hide abroad. Now they also wanted revenge. In 1399 Richard's cousin, Henry, returned with an army and forced Richard to give up being king. Henry became king. Soon afterwards Richard was murdered.

Quick History: who were the best kings in the Middle Ages?

So far you've investigated bad kings, poor kings and really awful kings. Now find out who were the best kings – with our tip-top set of Top Trumps cards!

ACTIVITY 1

1 On pages 121–123 are some 'King Top Trumps' cards. Divide up the cards amongst the class.
2 Look at the first two topics on your card: 'War' and 'Peace at home'. Add up the scores for just these two topics.
3 Now place your king on the life-line so you can see who did best and who did worst.

> ### WILLIAM I
> ### (the Conqueror)
> ### 1066–1087
> (died aged 59)
> **NORMAN**
>
> | **War:** | 10 |
> | Defeated rivals in France and conquered England | |
> | **Peace at home:** | 4 |
> | Lots of rebellions in England though he punished rebels savagely | |
> | **Famous for:** | 10 |
> | Battle of Hastings; Domesday Book; building castles | |
> | **Dramatic death:** | 7 |
> | Killed by his horse – it reared up and rammed the iron pommel on the saddle into William's stomach | |

4 a) Who were the top five kings?
  b) What made these kings such a success?

ACTIVITY 2

Divide into teams. Use the Top Trumps cards to solve these puzzles.

5 **Which king ...?**
  a) died applauding the archer who shot him?
  b) invented the handkerchief?
  c) built stone crosses in memory of his wife?
  d) was killed by his horse?
  e) lost the Crown jewels in The Wash?

6 **Quiz time!**
  a) How many kings were there in the thirteenth century?
  b) In which century did King Stephen reign?
  c) What do the years 1066 and 1483 have in common?

d) Put the following kings in date order:

Henry III   Edward I   John   William I   Richard III

e) Put the following dynasties in order
  York   Norman   Lancaster   Angevin
  Plantagenet   Tudor

7 **Odd ones out?**
  a) Edward II   Richard II   Henry V   Henry VI
  b) Arthur   Eustace   Peter   Alphonso
  c) Edward I   Edward III   Richard II   Henry V
  d) Henry II   Edward III   Richard I   John

WILLIAM II (Rufus)

1087–1100 **NORMAN**
(died aged 40)

War: 6
Won battles in France and Wales and won Cumbria from the Scots

Peace at home: 7
Worked well with his lords so few rebellions

Famous for: 3
Red face and hair; bad language and cruelty

Dramatic death: 8
Shot by an arrow while hunting. Probably an accident but it could have been murder organised by his brother Henry

HENRY I

1100–1135 **NORMAN**
(died aged 67)

War: 8
Won back Normandy from his brother Robert

Peace at home: 8
Improved government and kept peace through ruthless violence

Famous for: 2
Keeping one brother in prison for life and possibly murdering the other, William II

Dramatic death: 2
Went hunting all day aged 67, then ate too many eels and collapsed

STEPHEN

1135–1154 **NORMAN**
(died aged 58)

War: 1
A good soldier but not ruthless enough

Peace at home: 0
Civil war against his cousin Matilda and her son, Henry, lasted almost all his reign. England in chaos. He lost

Famous for: 2
Calling his eldest son Eustace. Fortunately Eustace never became king

Dramatic death: 0
In bed, defeated

HENRY II

1154–1189 **ANGEVIN**
(died aged 56)

War: 7
Ruled a huge empire energetically and kept control. Invaded Ireland

Peace at home: 6
Made lots of good laws but had to fight rebellions by his son

Famous for: 6
Terrible temper; murder of Becket

Dramatic death: 2
Died in bed during a war against his sons. When Richard, the eldest, came to see Henry's body, blood gushed from his nose

RICHARD I (the Lionheart)

1189–1199 **ANGEVIN**
(died aged 42)

War: 9
A magnificent soldier on Crusade, defeated all enemies at home

Peace at home: 7
Richard spent little time in England and rebellions broke out in his absence

Famous for: 8
Fighting; Crusading and nearly capturing Jerusalem; being held prisoner on his way home

Dramatic death: 10
He saw an archer shoot at him and applauded the shot, but didn't move out of the way of the arrow

JOHN (Lackland or Soft-sword)

1199–1216 **ANGEVIN**
(died aged 49)

War: 1
Lost the French empire. Did well in Wales

Peace at home: 2
He worked hard but quarrelled with the bishops and the barons, which led to civil war and a French invasion

Famous for: 8
Magna Carta; losing the Crown jewels

Dramatic death: 5
Ate too much, drank too much, got dysentery, died

HENRY III

1216–1272 **ANGEVIN**
(died aged 65)

War: 3
No great victories and no great losses

Peace at home: 2
Quarrelled with his barons led by Simon de Montfort and this started a civil war

Famous for: 2
Holding the first Parliaments; keeping an elephant and a polar bear in the Tower of London

Dramatic death: 0
Died in bed, very boring

EDWARD I (Longshanks)

1272–1307 **PLANTAGENET**
(died aged 68)

War: 8
Conquered Wales, battered the Scots, beat the French and even went on Crusade

Peace at home: 9
Nobody dared cause trouble. Called his eldest son Alphonso, but Al died young

Famous for: 7
Fighting! Winning the civil war for his father; being so sad he built 12 stone crosses to mark where his wife's body had rested on the way to her funeral

Dramatic death: 3
Died of illness on campaign against the Scots

EDWARD II PLANTAGENET

1307–1327
(Died aged 43)

War: 0
So bad he was beaten by the Scots at Bannockburn. He preferred farming to warfare

Peace at home: 1
Got on badly with his nobles and this led to civil wars until his wife and her lover put him in prison and took over ruling the country

Famous for: 4
Losing to the Scots and being horribly murdered

Dramatic death: 8
Murdered – perhaps with a red hot poker, although a rumour said he escaped and lived abroad as a monk

---

EDWARD III PLANTAGENET

1327–1377
(Died aged 65)

War: 8
Won famous victories over the French and Scots, but things went wrong in his last few years

Peace at home: 7
Made the country more peaceful and no civil wars – and he couldn't do anything about the Black Death

Famous for: 5
Winning battles such as Crécy and Poitiers

Dramatic death: 2
Died of old age. As he lay dying, his rings were stolen from his fingers by his lover, Alice Perrers

---

RICHARD II PLANTAGENET

1377–1399
(Died aged 32)

War: 1
French troops burned English towns while he tried to make peace

Peace at home: 1
He distrusted his nobles and this led to civil wars

Famous for: 3
Bravely ending the Peasants' Revolt in 1381: inventing the handkerchief

Dramatic death: 7
Probably murdered in Pontefract Castle on the orders of his cousin who had taken the Crown

---

HENRY IV LANCASTER

1399–1413
(Died aged 47)

War: 4
Went on Crusade to Russia; fought well against Welsh rebels but no other successes

Peace at home: 3
Civil wars and rebellion after he took the throne

Famous for: 2
Being the first king since 1066 who spoke English as his first language

Dramatic death: 6
A prophecy said he would die in Jerusalem. He collapsed in Westminster Abbey, then came round, asking 'Where am I?' When told 'In the Jerusalem Chamber', he died

---

HENRY V 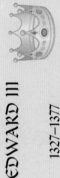 LANCASTER

1413–1422
(Died aged 35)

War: 9
Dramatic victory over French at Agincourt; conquered half of France

Peace at home: 9
Forced lords to obey laws – or else!

Famous for: 9
Agincourt, made by Shakespeare into a great play and then into films

Dramatic death: 4
Died of dysentery, still fighting the French

HENRY VI LANCASTER

1422–1461
(Died aged 50)

War: 0
Lost all the lands Henry V had won

Peace at home: 1
Useless king – lawlessness turned into civil wars called the Wars of the Roses

Famous for: 3
Becoming king aged nine months; being slightly mad and the only king deposed twice

Dramatic death: 7
Murdered in the Tower on Edward IV's orders

EDWARD IV YORK

1461–1483
(Died aged 40)

War: 5
Invaded France but took money to go away without fighting

Peace at home: 5
Bad start when civil war put doddery Henry VI back on the throne, but did a lot better when he won back the Crown

Famous for: 4
Being tall, blond and handsome; a brilliant soldier; lazy, drinking and eating too much

Dramatic death: 3
Died after going out fishing. Left young son to take over – a mistake

---

EDWARD V YORK

April–June 1483
(probably died aged 12)

War: 0
No time to fight anybody

Peace at home: 0
No time to rule the country

Famous for: 8
Disappearing along with his brother – known as the Princes in the Tower, they became one of the great murder mysteries in history

Dramatic death: 10
Nobody knows – were they really murdered by their uncle Richard?

RICHARD III 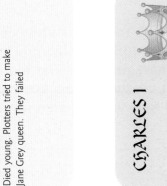 YORK

1483–1485
(Died aged 32)

War: 5
Frightened Scots and French so much they sent troops to help Henry Tudor depose him

Peace at home: 4
Could have been good but taking the Crown from his nephew caused rebellions

Famous for: 10
Murdering people – although he didn't do most (all?) of the murders the Tudors said he did

Dramatic death: 8
The last English king to be killed in battle, at Bosworth

HENRY VII TUDOR

1485–1509
(Died aged 52)

War: 7
Avoided wars and made alliances to keep England secure

Peace at home: 4
Struggled to stop rebellions but eventually made the country more peaceful

Famous for: 5
Being the first Tudor king; his eldest son Arthur died young, leaving another Henry to be king

Dramatic death: 0
Died in bed

HENRY VIII TUDOR

1509–1547
(Died aged 55)

War: 3
His generals beat the Scots for him, but he himself failed dismally against France

Peace at home: 3
Peaceful at first but closing the monasteries and changing the country's religion led to rebellions and significant long-term problems

Famous for: 10
Six wives; executing two, and numerous friends; destroying all the monasteries; being unpleasant and selfish

Dramatic death: 0
Died in bed

EDWARD VI TUDOR

1547–1553
(Died aged 15)

War: 3
Armies beat Scots

Peace at home: 1
Religious changes caused rebellions

Famous for: 3
Only son of Henry VIII; very religious and got rid of statues, colour and decorations in churches. A royal vandal!

Dramatic death: 2
Died young. Plotters tried to make Jane Grey queen. They failed

MARY TUDOR

1553–1558
(Died aged 42)

War: 1
Lost Calais, last English town in France

Peace at home: 3
Surprisingly few rebellions when she changed country's religion. Twenty per cent of people died from influenza and poverty after poor harvests

Famous for: 5
Made everyone become Catholic and executed over 300 people by burning who refused. Therefore known as 'Bloody Mary'

Dramatic death: 0
May have died of influenza

ELIZABETH I TUDOR

1558–1603
(Died aged 69)

War: 9
Stayed at peace as long as she could. Beat Spanish Armada

Peace at home: 7
Some religious rebellions but they had little support

Famous for: 10
Not marrying and being the 'Virgin Queen'; Executing Mary, Queen of Scots; beating Armada; not persecuting people over their religion

Dramatic death: 0
Died in bed peacefully

JAMES I STUART

1603–1625
(Died aged 59)

War: 5
Preferred peace to war but involved in religious wars

Peace at home: 8
Gunpowder Plot failed; peaceful

Famous for: 7
Being James VI of Scotland and King of England; united England and Scotland; nearly blown up by Gunpowder Plot; King James Bible; very messy eater

Dramatic death: 0
Died in bed

CHARLES I STUART

1625–1649
(Died aged 48)

War: 0
Too busy fighting his own people

Peace at home: 0
Tried to rule without Parliament for 11 years; this led to the Civil War

Famous for: 9
Bravery when executed; belief that God gave him Divine Right to rule; not keeping his word

Dramatic death: 10
Executed after being convicted of treason against his own people

THE BIG STORY: Power Part One

By the end of Key Stage 3 you'll be able to tell the story of power – who ruled Britain – all the way from the kings and barons in the Middle Ages to the struggles of ordinary people to win the right to vote in the nineteenth and twentieth centuries. This section has focused on the king and the barons. Now you can sum up what you've learned in one diagram.

My most important tasks as king are…

My biggest fear is…

People think I can do whatever I like but…

My barons will obey me if…

LEARNING LOG

You started this diagram on page 105. Now complete the thought bubbles to sum up the power of the King in the Middle Ages. You can add as many thought bubbles as you want and change any of the words. If you use your own words you are more likely to remember it when you begin Part Two of the Story of Power!

ACTIVITY

Discuss: Look back to where you placed Henry II on the power line on page 105. Do you think kings moved more to the left, more to the right or stayed in the same place through the Middle Ages?

1 A king's main jobs were to lead his army and to keep law and order

In the Middle Ages having an army and being a good fighter made someone powerful. A king was expected to be a great general and fighter, leading his men into battle and inspiring his soldiers with his bravery. Richard the Lionheart was a good example, leading successful cavalry charges in the Crusades.

3 Rebellions only happened if the barons were unhappy with the King

People believed that God chose the King and so rebelling against him was a very big risk to take – it seemed like rebelling against God. But even so, rebellions did happen when a king made big mistakes: if he lost an important war, or did not consult the important barons for advice, or gave all the rewards to his favourites.

5 Parliament had started but it was not very powerful

Regular Parliaments started with Edward I meeting his barons, knights and rich townsmen in the 1280s. Edward held Parliaments to get everyone to agree to taxes for his wars. But he didn't let Parliament take decisions. If Parliament tried to cause trouble the King just closed it down. Edward was such a good soldier nobody dared to challenge him.

2 A king could do more or less what he wanted – as long as the most powerful barons supported him

The King governed the country with the help of his most powerful barons. If the King was a great soldier, trusted his barons, rewarded them and took their advice, they supported him whatever he did. These kings made their barons feel like a 'band of brothers'. A King who had the support of his barons could do more or less what he liked – raise high taxes, go to war, quarrel with the Pope – with no fear of rebellion. The King and barons working together were just too powerful for anyone else to challenge them.

4 Nobody could imagine a country without a king

Remember King John. The rebellion was all about how he ruled. The barons didn't want to get rid of him. They just wanted him to rule properly. Magna Carta was a set of rules about how to govern the country. Even when the barons deposed a king the new king was a close relative of the last one. Nobody could imagine a country without a king.

6 Ordinary people did not have any power

Ordinary people did not help choose the King. They did not take part in Parliament. Their job was to work in the fields, pay taxes and do what they were told by their lords. Kings were not expected to make sure ordinary people had enough to eat or lived in good houses. Many people did not even have the right to leave their village to find work somewhere else.

> But that's about to change – as you'll find out in Section 5. We want to be free!

125

You are now going to study what life was like for ordinary people living hundreds of years ago in the Middle Ages. Was it comfortable, peaceful, boring, dangerous? Your big task will be to design a new history theme park based on a medieval village.

Welcome to Wharram Percy

This reconstruction drawing shows the village of Wharram Percy in Yorkshire as it might have looked in the early fourteenth century. The drawing is based on evidence found by archaeologists.

Most people in England lived in small villages like this – a group of houses, surrounded by fields and gardens and woodland. There were thousands all over England. Each village had a lord who had been given the land by the King. Most villagers worked for the lord.

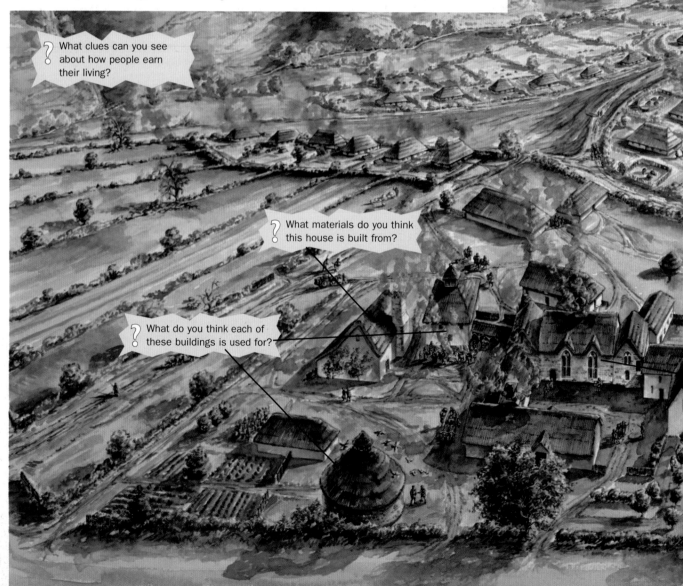

? What clues can you see about how people earn their living?

? What materials do you think this house is built from?

? What do you think each of these buildings is used for?

Where do you think they got their water?

Do you think life in this village looks comfortable or harsh?

List three differences between life in this village and life today.

How good is this road?

Who do you think lived in this large house?

ACTIVITY

1 Look closely at the picture. Discuss the questions that are scattered around.
2 What other questions do you have about this village?
3 Do you think life in Wharram Percy looks pleasant or harsh? Complete a table like this. Write as many points as you can under each heading.

Reasons why life in Wharram Percy might be pleasant	Reasons why life in Wharram Percy might be harsh

Discuss:
4 The owners of the history theme park want to call it 'Muck and Misery in the Middle Ages'. They think that will really pull in the visitors.
   a) Do you think it is a good name?
   b) Do think the evidence on this page fits that name?
5 Do you think this village changed during the Middle Ages or stayed much the same for 500 years? Give reasons for your choice and write them down. You'll come back to this question later!

▼ *This is the village viewed from another angle. Can you work out where you would stand to see this view?*

True or false?

START

ACTIVITY 1

1 Here's a fun activity on medieval life. Use your speed research to work out which of these 12 statements are true and which are false. You have 10 minutes to answer as many as you can, using pages 134–153 to help you. You will have to skim the pages quickly to find the information you need.

7. People had to ask the lord for permission to leave the village or to marry.

6. Kings kept elephants and polar bears in the Tower of London.

8. People were much shorter than we are nowadays.

9. You could be fined for throwing rubbish into the streets.

10. When the harvest was really bad people starved to death.

1. People believed the Earth was flat.

2. Football was banned by law.

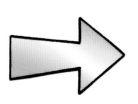

STRICTLY NO FOOTBALL BY LAW

3. People wore spectacles to help them read.

5. People did not have soap and they hardly ever had baths.

4. It was impossible for doctors to perform surgery. If they tried the patient always died.

12. Doctors tasted their patients' urine to decide what illnesses they had.

PATIENT SAMPLE

FINISH

11. Dick Whittington, who was the Lord Mayor of London a few times, gave the money to build a 128-seater toilet for Londoners to use.

TOILETS 128 SEATS

DONATED BY DICK WHITTINGTON, LORD MAYOR OF LONDON

ACTIVITY 2

Discuss:

2 What have you learned from this activity that:
  a) really interests you?
  b) really surprises you? Give reasons.

3 Which evidence:
  a) supports   **b)** challenges
calling the theme park 'Muck and Misery in the Middle Ages'?

The history theme park challenge!

Now it's time to start serious work on the history theme park. The owners, Botchit and Leggit, have recruited you to make it a success. They want it to be interesting. They want it to be fun. They **don't** care about it being historically accurate but **we** do. Can you meet the challenge and make it interesting, fun **and** accurate?

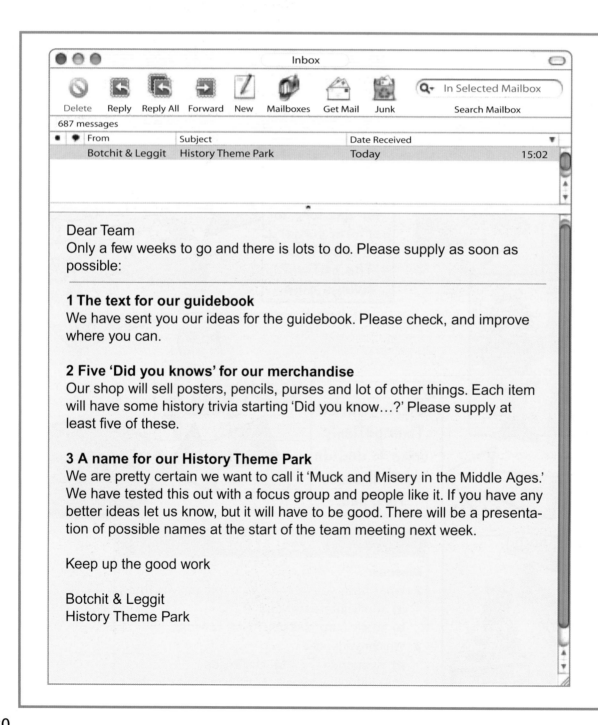

Dear Team
Only a few weeks to go and there is lots to do. Please supply as soon as possible:

1 The text for our guidebook
We have sent you our ideas for the guidebook. Please check, and improve where you can.

2 Five 'Did you knows' for our merchandise
Our shop will sell posters, pencils, purses and lot of other things. Each item will have some history trivia starting 'Did you know…?' Please supply at least five of these.

3 A name for our History Theme Park
We are pretty certain we want to call it 'Muck and Misery in the Middle Ages.' We have tested this out with a focus group and people like it. If you have any better ideas let us know, but it will have to be good. There will be a presentation of possible names at the start of the team meeting next week.

Keep up the good work

Botchit & Leggit
History Theme Park

ACTIVITY

That is your brief from Botchit and Leggit. Here is how to work.

For challenge 1 – the guidebook
Work in groups to check Botchit and Leggit's notes against the evidence files on pages 134–153. Everyone should do 'Fun' (so you get the idea of how to work). Then take two other topics each:
a) one of Homes, Farming, Towns and Travel, or Keeping Clean
b) one of Sickness, Punishments, Freedom, or Religion.
Your teacher will tell you which to do. You will share your research with others to produce a brilliant guidebook covering all the topics.

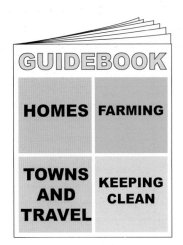

For challenge 2 – the 'Did you know' facts
As you work on the guidebook note down interesting facts – each on a separate card. Make sure they will fit on the merchandise like this:

Did you know...medieval kings kept polar bears in the Tower of London?

For challenge 3 – name the history theme park
Leave this until last. Make sure you are thoroughly familiar with as much evidence as possible. Then agree a name as a group. Make sure your name:
a) will attract visitors
b) gives a fair idea of life in the Middle Ages.
Prepare a short presentation to Botchit and Leggit to persuade them that your name is better than theirs.

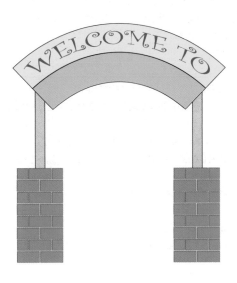

WELCOME TO

Botchit and Leggit's notes

FUN	People didn't have much fun in the Middle Ages. There was no sport. The only entertainments were singing and dancing. There were no books and nobody could read. They had no holidays apart from Sundays.
HOMES	Homes were very uncomfortable. They were poorly built from mud and bits of wood. People didn't improve their homes or clean them. Most people had hardly any clothes or valuables.
FARMING	Farmers had an awful life. They did all their work by hand. They had no machines. Men did not get any help from the women. Starvation was always just around the corner particularly after the Black Death in 1349, when everything got much worse.
TOWNS AND TRAVEL	Nobody ever left their village. There weren't many towns, and there was no reason to go to them anyway because there were no shops and no jobs. And they did not have good transport so no one wanted to travel round the country or go abroad.
KEEPING CLEAN	People were dirty and didn't worry about it. They never washed. They didn't try to keep their homes or streets clean. Nobody tried to be polite or have good manners.
SICKNESS	If you were sick you couldn't get any help. There were no doctors. None of their cures worked. Most people died very young.
PUNISHMENTS	Punishments were cruel and violent. Villagers caught criminals themselves. They decided if they were guilty by ducking them under water. People were hanged or had limbs cut off for even very minor crimes.
FREEDOM	People were not free. They had to work for their lords and do what the lords told them to do. They were not even allowed to leave their village without permission.
RELIGION	People did not care about religion. Priests just took the villagers' money then preached them sermons about hell. No wonder people did not go to church very often. They did not get any practical help from the priest.

Each topic has a big point and little points to support it. For example, on the topic of Fun, Botchit and Leggit say:

This is the Big Point

These are the Little Points

> People didn't have much fun in the Middle Ages.

> There was no sport.

> The only entertainments were singing and dancing. There were no books and nobody could read. They had no holidays apart from Sundays.

1 Now you can practise by checking the paragraph about Fun using the grid below and the evidence file on pages 134–135. Check each little point in turn.
Is each one right or wrong? What else can you find out? Fill in column 2 of the grid – we've started it for you.

B and L's little points about fun	What the evidence file says about each little point
a) *There was no sport*	This is wrong. They practised archery, and they played football.
b) *The only entertainments were singing and dancing*	They also told stories.
c) *There were no books and nobody could read*	
d) *They had no holidays apart from Sundays*	Christmas

2 Now use the completed grid to decide whether the Big Point is correct.

People didn't have much fun in the Middle Ages.

If you think it's wrong, rewrite the Big Point so it's correct.

3 Now put it all together and write a draft paragraph, using your Big Point and some improved little points, for a new guidebook that will give visitors to the theme park a better idea about Fun in the Middle Ages.

4 Finally:
   a) Create a **good final copy** of your paragraph.
   b) Choose **one picture** to illustrate it.
   c) Check the **spelling**.
   d) Make sure it's **interesting** to visitors.

Did people have fun in the Middle Ages?

Most of the pictures come from the Luttrell Psalter. This was a prayer book illustrated for Sir Geoffrey Luttrell around 1330. The illustrations show Sir Geoffrey, his servants and other people from his village in Lincolnshire.

ℹ️ **HOLY-DAYS**

In the Middle Ages people had plenty of days off work, probably more than many people today. They didn't work on Sundays or on religious days like Christmas and Easter, or on Saints' days – and there were plenty of those! So they had the religious days or 'holy-days' off work. Holy-day is the original word for holiday. The pictures on these pages show some of the things people could do on their holy-days.

▼ **PICTURE 1** *Archery practice*

ℹ️ **ARCHERY v. FOOTBALL**

The law stated that all men had to practise archery to keep them ready for war. However, many men enjoyed playing football and other ball games instead. The kings kept making laws banning football and ordering men to practise archery, but the laws didn't work as football was much more popular than archery.

ℹ️ **UNUSUAL ANIMALS**

There were plenty of wolves and bears in Britain, but sometimes people would have seen more unusual animals. For example, the kings of England were often given wild animals as presents by the rulers of other countries. Henry III kept leopards, an elephant and a polar bear at the Tower of London. The polar bear went swimming in the River Thames on the end of a very long lead! In the 1430s two of the King's officials took the King's ostrich to Norwich. They charged people to see the ostrich in a special tent, but they were beaten up three times by people who objected to paying.

▶ **PICTURE 2** *Bear baiting*

▼ **PICTURE 3** *Drunk!*

i **ALE OR WINE?**

Only rich people drank wine. The poor man's drink was ale, a kind of very weak beer. People drank ale because they knew that water often became dirty and made people ill. Ale was brewed by the women in each village.

▼ **PICTURE 4** *Hawking*

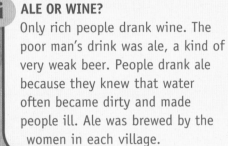

i **TRAVELLING ENTERTAINERS**
These people would perform in the villages and people would dance and sing. There were also travelling wrestlers, acrobats and jugglers, and storytellers who would tell tales of Robin Hood or King Arthur.

▶ **PICTURE 5**
Travelling musicians

i **HUNTING WITH HAWKS**
Only rich people could afford to own hawks. Hawks and hunting equipment were often given as presents.

Were homes uncomfortable in the Middle Ages?

ACTIVITY

The Big Point in Botchit and Leggit's notes is:

Homes were very uncomfortable.

1 Use the information on these two pages to check if the little points in the grid are correct.

B and L's little points about homes	What the evidence file says about each little point
a) They were poorly built from mud and bits of wood.	
b) People didn't improve their homes or clean them.	
c) Most people had hardly any clothes or valuables.	

2 Now think about the Big Point about Homes. If you think it's wrong, rewrite the Big Point so it's correct.

3 Follow steps **3** and **4** from page 133 to complete your paragraph about Homes.

EVIDENCE FILE: Homes

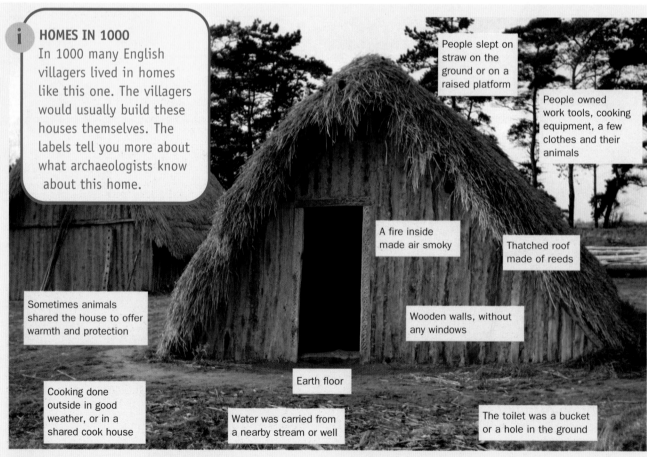

i HOMES IN 1000
In 1000 many English villagers lived in homes like this one. The villagers would usually build these houses themselves. The labels tell you more about what archaeologists know about this home.

People slept on straw on the ground or on a raised platform

People owned work tools, cooking equipment, a few clothes and their animals

A fire inside made air smoky

Thatched roof made of reeds

Sometimes animals shared the house to offer warmth and protection

Wooden walls, without any windows

Cooking done outside in good weather, or in a shared cook house

Earth floor

Water was carried from a nearby stream or well

The toilet was a bucket or a hole in the ground

▲ **PICTURE 6** *Reconstructed Anglo-Saxon house at West Stow. Find out more at www.stedmundsbury.gov*

WEALTHY HOMES

The homes of the wealthy changed even more. They were built of stone or brick and had fireplaces, chimneys and toilets. They had glass windows instead of wooden shutters and the floors were tiled. These homes had two floors and separate bedrooms.

ⓘ **HOMES IN 1500**

The homes of ordinary people changed during the Middle Ages – particularly those of better-off villagers. By 1500 some villagers were building homes like this one, which is still standing at a museum in Kent. It was built by professional carpenters or builders. In 1500 it had only one floor – the top floor was added later. The labels tell you more about what archaeologists know about this home.

▼ **PICTURE 7** *A house built in the late 1400s, now standing at the Downland Museum in Kent. Find out more at www.wealddown.co.uk*

Furniture included a raised bed, a wardrobe, chairs, a lockable casket for money

Possessions included colourful clothes, pottery jugs with nice patterns, tablecloths, candle holders and oil lamps

Shutters on the windows (but still no glass)

Iron locks on the door

Water came from the nearby well but the house had a garde-robe (toilet)

Herbs were placed in the bed to keep away insects

Separate rooms for sleeping and eating

Stone base to help stop damp spreading, with a wooden floor on top which was kept well swept

Animals kept in separate barns, which looked much like the 1100 human houses

Did farmers have a hard life?

ACTIVITY

The Big Point in Botchit and Leggit's notes is:

> **Farmers had an awful life.**

1 Use the information on these two pages to check if the little points in the grid are correct.

B and L's little points about farming	What the evidence file says about each little point
a) *They did all their farm work by hand.*	
b) *Men did not get any help from the women.*	
c) *Starvation was always just around the corner – particularly after the Black Death.*	

2 Now think about the Big Point about Farming. If you think it's wrong, rewrite the Big Point so it's correct.

3 Follow steps **3** and **4** from page 133 to complete your paragraph about Farming.

EVIDENCE FILE: Farming

ⓘ **LIFE OR DEATH**

Throughout the Middle Ages, the weather was life or death to ordinary people. Over 90 per cent of people were farmers and their lives depended on how good the harvest was each summer. If it was too cold or there was too much rain, the harvest was poor and people went hungry. Today, we can import food from abroad or send it long distances from one part of the country to another, but they could not. So, if the harvest was poor for two or three years running, food ran out and some people starved to death. But this was rare. Most of the time the system worked.

ⓘ **WOMEN'S WORK**

Every woman, from ordinary villagers to ladies in their castles, had a spinning wheel in her home. They spun the wool from their sheep into thread and then used the thread to weave cloth for clothes or blankets. This was as well as all their other work.

▲ PICTURE 9 *Spinning*

The pictures are from the Luttrell Psalter (see page 134).

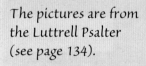

▶ **PICTURE 8** *Milking*

▲ **PICTURE 10** *Ploughing*

i | **TOOLS AND MACHINES**
The plough was the nearest thing to a machine. It was pulled by oxen and was steered by hand. The seed was scattered by hand and clumps of soil were broken up by hitting them with mallets (clod-breaking). This was exhausting work!

◀ **PICTURE 11** *Clod-breaking*

i | **THE LORD'S WORK** As well as farming their own land, people usually had to spend at least two days a week looking after the land belonging to their lord.

i | **WAGES**
This graph shows how wages changed during the Middle Ages. The big rise you can see is because of the Black Death. It killed nearly 50 per cent of the population in 1349 so there were not enough people to farm the land. Those who survived earned higher wages. This meant that more ordinary people could afford better food, more clothes and to send their children to school.

i | **HARVEST TIME** Everyone worked in the fields – men, women and children. They did the harvesting on their hands and knees. The corn was cut with a scythe. After the corn had been carried away the women and children went round picking up every last piece of corn. Nothing could be wasted.

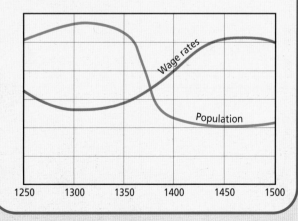

◀ **PICTURE 12** *Harvest time*

139

Were towns worth visiting?

ACTIVITY 1

The Big Point in Botchit and Leggit's notes is:

> Nobody ever left their village.

1 Use the information on the next four pages to check if the little points in the grid are correct.

B and L's little points about towns and travel	What the evidence file says about each little point
a) *There weren't many towns.*	
b) *There were no shops in towns.*	
c) *There were no jobs in towns.*	
d) *They did not have good transport.*	

2 Now think about the Big Point about towns and travel. If you think it's wrong, rewrite the Big Point so it's correct.

3 Follow steps **3** and **4** from page 133 to complete your paragraph about Towns and Travel.

EVIDENCE FILE: Towns

i HOW MANY?

In 1066, 10 per cent of people in England lived in towns. By 1300 this figure had risen to 20 per cent. There were only 100 towns in 1066. There were over 800 towns in 1300. The map shows the largest. London was the only big town. In 1300 it had 100,000 people.

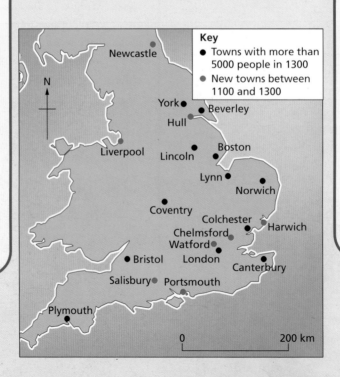

i WHAT WAS A TOWN?

A village had to apply to the King for the right to become a town. Being a town gave special privileges such as the right to hold markets, which made the townspeople a lot of money. Townspeople had to pay taxes to the King for these privileges.

i **LINCOLN IN 1100**
It is really no more than a large village. The townspeople grew their crops in the fields nearby.

▲ PICTURE 13 *Artist's impression of Lincoln in 1100.*

▼ PICTURE 14 *Artist's impression of Lincoln in 1500.*

ACTIVITY 2

4 Find five similarities and five differences between the two pictures.

i **LINCOLN IN 1500** Lincoln had three markets a week and a huge fair once a year. People from nearby villages often visited Lincoln to sell surplus food from their harvest or to buy cloth or pottery dishes. You could visit a goldsmith, baker or fishmonger, or buy clothes, leather shoes, or sugar and spices.

141

Travel

Use this evidence file to help you with the task on page 140.

▶ **PICTURE 15A**
A map of London to Dover originally drawn by Matthew Paris in the thirteenth century.

▼ **PICTURE 15B** *A copy of part of the Gough map. Drawn in about 1360, it shows 2,940 miles of roads, but only the main carrier routes in England and Wales are shown below. There were many more roads in the North and Scotland. We do not know who drew the map. Some of the routes are on the same lines as the old Roman roads.*

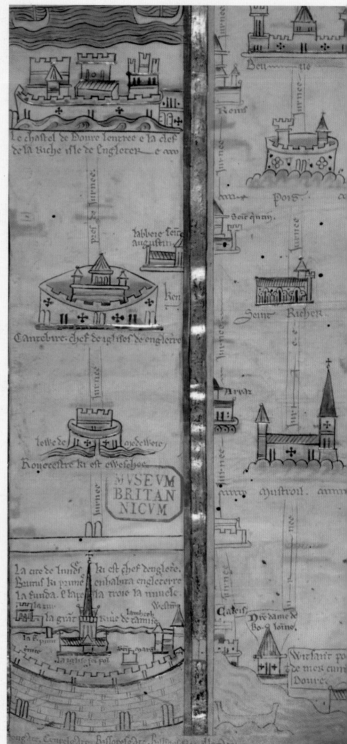

142

▼ **PICTURE 16** *Three pictures from the* Luttrell Psalter *showing different methods of travel.*

ⓘ **TRAVELLING ON FOOT**
A lot of people travelled on foot. Some freemen travelled great distances to go on pilgrimage to countries such as Spain – and they walked every step of the way.

ⓘ **TRAVELLING BY CART**
Because many people travelled to town fairs to sell their goods, carts were often used. There were even cart-parks at the fair!

ⓘ **TRAVELLING BY HORSE**
Those that were rich enough could travel by horse allowing them to travel long distances quickly.

ⓘ Don't believe anyone who says people in the Middle Ages thought the world was flat. They didn't. They always knew it was round!

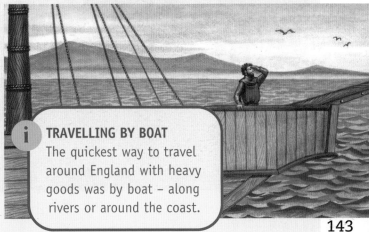

ⓘ **TRAVELLING BY BOAT**
The quickest way to travel around England with heavy goods was by boat – along rivers or around the coast.

Did people try to keep clean?

ACTIVITY

The Big Point in Botchit and Leggit's notes is:

> **People were dirty and didn't worry about it.**

1 Use the information on these two pages to check if the little points in the grid are correct.

B and L's little points about keeping clean	What the evidence file says about each little point
a) *They never washed.*	
b) *They didn't try to keep their homes or streets clean.*	
c) *Nobody tried to be polite or have good manners.*	

2 Now think about the Big Point about Keeping clean. If you think it's wrong, rewrite the Big Point so it's correct.

3 Follow steps **3** and **4** from page 133 to complete your paragraph about Keeping clean.

EVIDENCE FILE: Keeping clean

BATHS, SOAP AND TOOTHPASTE

The rich were able to have baths regularly. Baths were often made from wooden wine casks.

Soap was made by boiling sheep fat in wood ash and caustic soda. People also cleaned their teeth, using a springy hazel twig. Both rich and poor would have soap and hazel twigs.

All water had to be fetched by hand, and hot water needed to be boiled on a fire, so it was used carefully.

▲ **PICTURE 17** *Bath time! An illustration from a medieval manuscript.*

GOOD MANNERS

Around 1200 a man called Daniel of Beccles wrote *The Book of the Civilised Man*. He gave advice to people on how to behave politely. Here is a small part of his advice. This book would only be bought by rich people, but the advice applied to anyone who wanted to be civilised.

WHEN YOU ARE IN PUBLIC
· *Do not eat in the street.*
· *Do not scratch yourself.*
· *Do not look for fleas on your trousers or hair.*
· *Do not comb your hair or clean your nails.*
· *Do not take your shoes off in front of lords and ladies.*

WHEN YOU ARE EATING
· *Cut up your food into small portions with your knife.*
· *Pick up your food with your thumb and index finger only.* (Forks were not invented until around 1400.)
· *Do not lick your fingers, or pick your teeth, or talk with your mouth full, or put your elbows on the table, or pick your nose.*
· *Do not let pigs or cats into the hall although dogs and hawks are allowed.*
· *Turn round if you have to spit on the floor.*
· *Do not urinate in the hall unless you are the lord.* (Lords got a servant to bring a jug to the table so they didn't have to leave the room to urinate.)

EVIDENCE FROM TOWNS

The best evidence for whether people tried to keep clean comes from towns. They were probably dirtier than villages because there were more people. York is a good example and it has been well researched by archaeologists.

▼ **PICTURE 18** *This eleventh-century street in York has been reconstructed in the Jorvik museum. It looked very different by 1500.*

In the eleventh century, York was a filthy place.

- Pigs, chickens and other animals roamed the streets.
- Rats and mice, hawks and falcons scavenged amidst the rubbish.
- Wicker-lined pits were used as toilets or rubbish bins but no one emptied them regularly.
- The streets were full of rotting fish bones, animal dung, food waste and even human faeces.
- Water for drinking and cooking was collected from the river or from storage pits, which were often next to the cesspits that people used as toilets.

Two hundred years later, York was much cleaner.

- Many houses had stone foundations.
- Some houses were built entirely of stone.
- Cesspits were lined with brick or stone and so did not leak into drinking water.
- Sewers were built to take waste away from the city.
- The biggest problem was keeping the streets clean because people rode horses the way we use cars – and the horses made a mess in the streets! So did the cattle, sheep and geese which arrived in towns every week to be butchered for food.

In other towns similar changes were taking place.

In fourteenth-century London, for example, the fine for throwing litter into the street was two shillings. That was two weeks' wages for a farm worker. Anyone who left lots of rubbish outside their house was fined four shillings. Public toilets and sewers were built to keep London clean. Richard (Dick) Whittington, who was Lord Mayor of London four times, built a public toilet with 128 seats, 64 for men and 64 for women.

Could they help the sick?

ACTIVITY

The Big Point in Botchit and Leggit's notes is:

> If you were sick you couldn't get any help.

a) Make a grid about the little points from the notes on Sickness on page 132.
b) Follow steps **1** to **4** from page 133 to complete your paragraph about Sickness.

IF YOU FELT ILL ...

... you could turn to your family

Most illnesses were treated by women and members of the family. Women knew a lot of effective remedies made from flowers and herbs. Herbal remedies were often successful because people had learned which ones worked, even if they didn't know why. Honey was used to treat infections and today we know it contains ingredients that kill germs.

... if you were rich you could see a physician

Physicians studied medicine at university. A physician would:
- examine your urine – by colour, smell or taste
- tell you that your humours (the main liquids in your body) were out of balance. People believed that they became ill when their humours were out of balance
- take blood from your vein (bleeding) or purge you to empty your bowels – to re-balance the humours.

... you could see a barber-surgeon

Surgeons learned medicine by watching another surgeon. They could perform simple surgery and take blood from people (see Picture 20). Some surgeons could carry out complicated operations. This skull (Picture 21) belonged to a man who died aged about 40. He had been hit on the head, leaving splinters of bone in his brain. A surgeon peeled back the skin and cut away the splinters of bone. The man lived.

Mum, my head hurts!

▲ **PICTURE 19**
A physician's clinic.

▲ **PICTURE 20** *A barber-surgeon bleeding a patient.*

OLD AGE

Most people died before the age of 50, but good food and less work meant that the rich could hope to live past 60.

WELL FED?

Fact: well fed and healthy children grow into taller adults. We know from excavations of medieval graves that the average height of women was 1.6 metres and was 1.7 metres for men. That's taller than people in the 1800s! What do you make of that?

... you could pray, and ask God to help

People were very religious. They believed that illnesses might be caused by evil spirits or be God's punishment for wrong deeds, so praying was a good way of getting better. You could pray whether you were rich or poor.

NOT MUCH CHANGE

Bleeding, purging and herbal remedies were the most common treatments in the Middle Ages. Some worked, but many illnesses could not be treated. Nobody understood that germs (bacteria) cause infectious diseases, so there was no way to stop diseases from spreading. You could die from infection if you cut your finger because there were no antibiotics.

DIET

Hard manual labour uses lots of energy. Farm workers could burn 4000 calories a day so they had to eat a lot. The average medieval peasant would have eaten every day: porridge and soup, two loaves of bread, 8oz (250g) of meat or fish, and vegetables including beans, turnips and parsnips. This was washed down with three pints of ale a day. There were no biscuits, cake or sweets. 'If you put this together with the incredible work they did, medieval people were at much less risk of heart disease than we are today' (Dr Henderson, an expert in medieval diet).

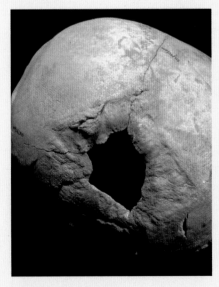

▲ **PICTURE 21**
Skull found at Wharram Percy.

Were punishments cruel and violent?

ACTIVITY

The Big Point in Botchit and Leggit's notes is:

Punishments were cruel and violent.

a) Make a grid about the little points from the notes on Punishments from page 132.

b) Follow steps **1** to **4** from page 133 to complete your paragraph about Punishments.

EVIDENCE FILE: Punishments

i CATCHING CRIMINALS

- There were no paid policemen in the Middle Ages.
- There were village constables. They were ordinary people who also had other jobs. They were not paid. They just kept watch when they could.
- If someone saw a crime, they raised the 'hue and cry'. This meant everyone else had to chase the criminal and try to catch them.
- If they caught the criminal and, if the crime was serious enough, the criminal was taken by the constable to the sheriff of the county, and kept in prison until a trial.

i TRIALS

If there were witnesses to a crime, a judge would find out from them what had happened. But what happened if there were no witnesses or if the witnesses disagreed?

Until 1215, people let God decide. The accused was taken into a church to face trial by ordeal. There were different kinds of ordeal.

- One was ordeal by hot iron. The accused had to carry a piece of burning hot iron for three metres. Then the hand was bandaged for three days before being unwrapped. If the hand was healing cleanly, it was believed that God was telling everyone that the person was innocent. If it was infected, he or she was guilty.
- Other ordeals involved plunging an arm into boiling water or lowering the accused into a river to see if they would sink or float.

Trial by ordeal was abolished in 1215. **After 1215**, all trials were decided by judges and juries. Juries were made up of ordinary people who probably knew the accused.

PUNISHMENTS

Prison was not used as a punishment. There were a few small jails in castles where some accused people were held until trial. But prisons were too expensive (they need guards and strong buildings). Instead, there were three main punishments used throughout the Middle Ages:

- **The stocks.** People threw rotten food (or worse) at you. This made you look foolish.

- **A fine.** For example, you could be fined a week's wages for letting your animals eat other villagers' crops.

- **Hanging.** Many people were hanged for stealing clothes or food. Executions took place in public as a warning to others to obey the law.

▲ PICTURE 22 *Illustration from a medieval manuscript showing a nun and a monk in the stocks.*

CASE STUDY: JOHN PETERSON – MURDERER!

One day in the early 1300s John Ballock broke into Emma Robb's house and stole two sides of bacon. Emma shouted out for help, starting the hue and cry. Everyone who heard her joined in the chase.

John Peterson chased the thief into a field, but Ballock drew his sword, swung it at Peterson and wounded him. Peterson had to defend himself. He hit Ballock on the head with his axe, killing him instantly.

Peterson was taken to the sheriff, who held him in prison until a court was held. The judge listened to the villagers who saw what happened. Then he decided whether Peterson was guilty or innocent. He was found guilty.

How do you think Peterson was punished? Write down your ideas. Your teacher can tell you the answer.

Were people free?

ACTIVITY

The Big Point in Botchit and Leggit's notes is:

> ## People were not free.

a) Make a grid about the little points from the notes on Freedom from page 132.

b) Follow steps **1** to **4** from page 133 to complete your paragraph about Freedom.

EVIDENCE FILE: Freedom

1300

i This is how society was organised 1100–1400. The higher up you were, the more power and freedom you had. It was almost impossible for people to move up the ladder and become wealthier and more powerful.

i Around 40 per cent of the villagers in England were not free. These people were called villeins. Villeins could only become free by buying their freedom or by running away to a town. If they stayed there for a year and a day the law said they were free. The lord could not take them back.

> I have to work on my lord's land for two days every week without pay.

> I need the lord's permission to leave the village or to let my daughter get married.

> I had to give the lord my best cow when I took over my father's land. At Easter we give him six eggs, a goose and a chicken.

KING

NOBLES

KNIGHTS

MERCHANTS

FREEMEN

VILLEINS

Feudal System 1100 – 1400

i **THE PASTON STORY PART 1: Ploughman and villein**

Clement Paston was born around 1350. He was a villein in the village of Paston in Norfolk. He spent his life as a ploughman, but he owned a horse that he rode (bareback) and (with the lord's permission) he also drove his horse-drawn cart to market to sell his surplus corn.

He married Beatrix Somerton who was also the daughter of a villein so they needed the permission of their lord to marry.

1500

This is how society was organised after 1400. It became easier for people to move up the ladder and become wealthier and more powerful.

By 1500 there were no **villeins**. Everyone was free. These great changes happened mainly because of two events you are going to study later – the Black Death, in 1348, and the Peasants' Revolt of 1381.

No more working without pay!

We can leave the village to find better paid work whenever we want. And there is no more asking permission for our daughters to get married.

No more payments when we take over land from our fathers.

KING

NOBLES

KNIGHTS

MERCHANTS

FREEMEN

VILLEINS

1400s

THE PASTON STORY PART 2: Lawyer and courtier

By the end of the fourteenth century Clement had become a free man. He could work for wages and was able to run his own affairs. He saved from his wages and also borrowed money from Beatrix's brother Geoffrey to send their son William to school.

William became a lawyer and a judge. He married Agnes Berry, the daughter of a knight, and bought land in different parts of Norfolk.

Their eldest son, John, became an MP and the owner of the castle at Caister – see Picture 23. Both his sons were knighted and became courtiers.

By the 1470s, just 100 years since Clement won his freedom, his great-grandsons were working in the King's household and mixing with the most powerful people in the country. That is what freedom did for the Paston family!

▲ **PICTURE 23** *Caister Castle in Norfolk, which became the Pastons' home in the 1460s.*

151

Were people religious in the Middle Ages?

ACTIVITY

The Big Point in Botchit and Leggit's notes is:

People did not care about religion.

a) Make a grid about the little points from the notes on Religion from page 132.
b) Follow steps **1** to **4** from page 133 to complete your paragraph about Religion.

i People believed that God created and controlled the world and everything in it. It was wrong to argue about the differences in society between rich and poor, or men and women, because God had created these differences.

All the pictures except picture 25 come from medieval manuscripts.

▼ **PICTURE 25** *A medieval mural on the wall of Chaldon church. Heaven is at the top, hell at the bottom.*

▲ **PICTURE 26** *A priest gives the sacrament to rich lords and ladies.*

▲ **PICTURE 24** *God is shown holding the world surrounded by worshipping angels.*

i People went to church every Sunday, on Saints' Days and festivals like Christmas. They believed that if they went to church and followed the Church's rules then they would go to Heaven when they died, and if they didn't they would go to Hell.

Thousands of people worked as monks, nuns and village priests. It was them, rather than the King or government who helped the poor and unemployed by providing money and food. They called this 'giving alms'.

The priest was one of the most important people in the village. He helped the poor and elderly and taught some children to read and write. In return villagers paid him a tithe (a tenth) of all their crops every year. The only way to be educated was to go to a church school.

▲ PICTURE 27 *A nun giving bread to poor people.*

◄ PICTURE 28 *A priest teaching children to read and write.*

▼ PICTURE 29 *Pilgrims being welcomed in Jerusalem.*

Many people went on pilgrimages to pray at holy places like the tomb of Thomas Becket at Canterbury. The greatest pilgrimage was to Jerusalem where Jesus Christ had lived and died. Pilgrims wore badges to show which holy places they had visited.

THE BIG STORY: Ordinary Life Part One

It will be clear to you from your work on the history theme park that some aspects of life changed a lot during the Middle Ages. Others changed very little. This page helps you get an overview. Then in Section 5 you will investigate why some of the changes happened.

No change

Small changes

Big and important changes

ACTIVITY

Use your completed guidebook to help you choose the right colour star.
- Red means there was no change in this topic in the Middle Ages.
- Yellow means there was some change in this topic in the Middle Ages.
- Green means there were important changes in this topic in the Middle Ages.

Which colour of sticker is the correct one to go in each square?

FUN

HOMES

FREEDOM

SICKNESS

PUNISHMENTS

TOWNS AND TRAVEL

KEEPING CLEAN

FARMING

RELIGION

154

DOING HISTORY: **Change and continuity**

Change and continuity

At any one time, there are usually things that are changing and things that stay the same (continuities)

① Refer to your Activity on page 154. What stayed the same in the Middle Ages?

② What changed in the Middle Ages?

Change and continuity

Some changes happen quickly. Some happen slowly

③ Give an example of one change in medieval life that happened quite quickly. (There's a clue in the picture above.)

LEARNING LOG

Everyday life is another Big Story you're going to follow through time. Your history theme park guidebook should be the perfect record of what you have learned so far. It should include all the big points about ordinary life in the Middle Ages along with evidence to back them up.

But do you want to improve that record before you move on? For example, turn it into a podcast or a make it into a PowerPoint or a movie?

Why did people in the Middle Ages love the stories about Robin Hood?

Robin Hood stories were very popular in the Middle Ages. They would be told as ballads (long songs sung by a storyteller). Here is a Robin Hood story that is at least 600 years old. Your task is to work out why it was so popular in the Middle Ages.

ACTIVITY

Before you read the story

1 Make a list of the things that make a story enjoyable for you.

2 If you have heard of Robin Hood, what do you expect to happen in a Robin Hood story?

3 Now think about what you have learned about the Middle Ages so far. What kind of story do you think would be popular with people in the Middle Ages?

After you read the story

4 Did you enjoy it? Why? Why not?

5 Is there anything in the story that surprises you? Explain what it is and why it surprises you.

6 Which of the ingredients you mentioned in question 3 are present in the story?

7 Why do *you* think it was such a popular story in the Middle Ages? List at least two reasons.

Robin Hood and the monk

> I have not been to church for two weeks.

> I swear by Him that died on the tree, I am as happy as anyone in the whole country!

It was a beautiful May morning in the forest. Little John couldn't have been happier but Robin was miserable.

Robin decided to go to a church service in Nottingham. Much, the Miller's son, told him he needed a guard of 20 men, but Robin said he would only take Little John.

On the way through the forest Robin and John had an archery contest, shooting at branches and bushes. John won.

Then Robin hit Little John and the two men fought. John pulled out his sword but would not use it against Robin. Robin continued to Nottingham alone.

In Nottingham Robin went to the Church of St Mary's. As he went in he was recognised by a monk.

The monk ran to the sheriff and told him Robin was in the church.

The town gates were closed and locked and the sheriff led his soldiers to the church.

The sheriff and his men attacked Robin. Robin drew his sword and killed twelve of them but broke his sword on the sheriff's armour.

Robin was captured and put in jail. The sheriff sent the monk with a letter giving the good news to the King.

Little John and Much heard that Robin was a prisoner and set out to rescue him. They decided to capture the monk first.

They seized the monk, cut off his head and killed his servant.

Bring Robin Hood to me for punishment.

Little John and Much found the sheriff's letter in the monk's bag and took it to the King themselves. He rewarded them well.

Then Little John and Much returned to Nottingham. They gave the sheriff the King's message. They even had dinner with the sheriff who fell asleep, drunk.

That night John and Much went to the jail and shouted 'Robin's escaped!' The jailer rushed out and they knocked him out.

Then they found Robin and released him from prison. They climbed over the town walls and escaped.

Back in the forest, Little John told Robin he was leaving. He had done Robin a good turn, despite Robin not paying him the five shillings for the archery contest, but now he wanted to leave.

Robin told John he wanted him to stay and offered to let John become leader.

John said he would not be leader, but decided to stay, and they celebrated with wine and roast deer.

The wonders of Baghdad –
what stories will you bring back?

Travel was much slower in the Middle Ages than it is today but that did not stop people from going anywhere. Merchants were the keenest travellers. They would travel in search of goods to bring back to sell in England. So imagine you are a medieval traveller. You are going to leave England and travel over 1,000 miles to the Muslim city of Baghdad. What will amaze you? You are going to write a diary about what you see.

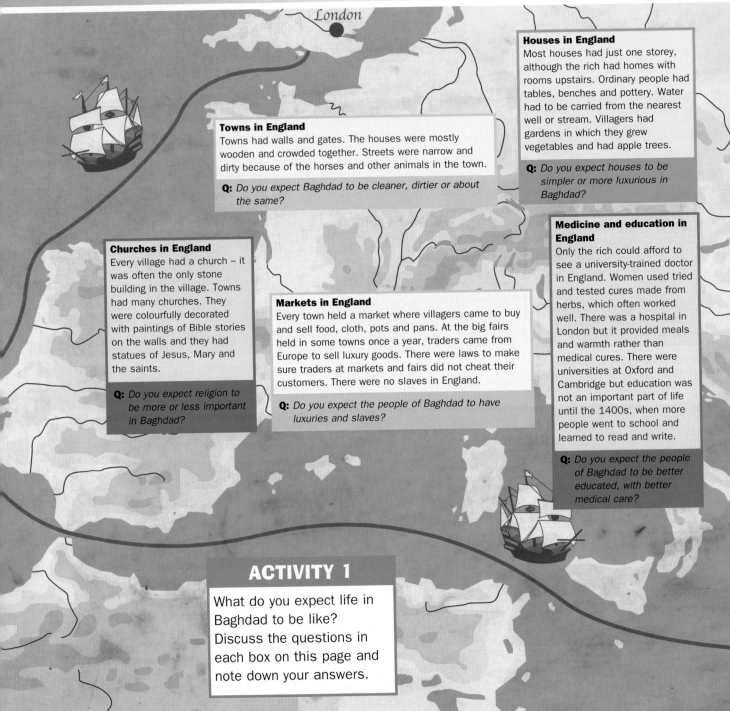

London

Houses in England
Most houses had just one storey, although the rich had homes with rooms upstairs. Ordinary people had tables, benches and pottery. Water had to be carried from the nearest well or stream. Villagers had gardens in which they grew vegetables and had apple trees.

Q: *Do you expect houses to be simpler or more luxurious in Baghdad?*

Towns in England
Towns had walls and gates. The houses were mostly wooden and crowded together. Streets were narrow and dirty because of the horses and other animals in the town.

Q: *Do you expect Baghdad to be cleaner, dirtier or about the same?*

Medicine and education in England
Only the rich could afford to see a university-trained doctor in England. Women used tried and tested cures made from herbs, which often worked well. There was a hospital in London but it provided meals and warmth rather than medical cures. There were universities at Oxford and Cambridge but education was not an important part of life until the 1400s, when more people went to school and learned to read and write.

Q: *Do you expect the people of Baghdad to be better educated, with better medical care?*

Churches in England
Every village had a church – it was often the only stone building in the village. Towns had many churches. They were colourfully decorated with paintings of Bible stories on the walls and they had statues of Jesus, Mary and the saints.

Q: *Do you expect religion to be more or less important in Baghdad?*

Markets in England
Every town held a market where villagers came to buy and sell food, cloth, pots and pans. At the big fairs held in some towns once a year, traders came from Europe to sell luxury goods. There were laws to make sure traders at markets and fairs did not cheat their customers. There were no slaves in England.

Q: *Do you expect the people of Baghdad to have luxuries and slaves?*

ACTIVITY 1

What do you expect life in Baghdad to be like? Discuss the questions in each box on this page and note down your answers.

ACTIVITY 2

1 Use a diary (like the one on the right) to record what you see as you explore the city of Baghdad. Each day you must record at least one thing that grabs your attention. It could be something:

- that amazes you because there's nothing like it at home
- that you wish you could copy at home to make life better
- that surprises you because it's just the same as at home.

Day 1	Day 2
The round city	Homes
Day 3	**Day 4**
Streets and markets	Libraries and doctors

Remember

You are moving:
- from an English <u>village</u> to a Middle Eastern <u>city</u>
- from English weather to desert heat
- from a Christian country to a Muslim country.

2 At the end of your visit you will choose the thing you think was most memorable and explain why you chose it.

Constantinople

Baghdad

Jerusalem

The round city

Baghdad was the capital city of the Abbasid Muslim Empire. It had been built from scratch, starting in 762. Workers were sent from every city in the empire to build the new capital. At the centre was the round city, built in the shape of a circle with an outer wall and two inner walls, and a deep moat for defence. The city was magnificent. The palace had a golden gate and a green dome more than 30 metres high. It was right next to the main mosque so that when people bowed down to pray they were also bowing down to the Caliph.

Ⓐ

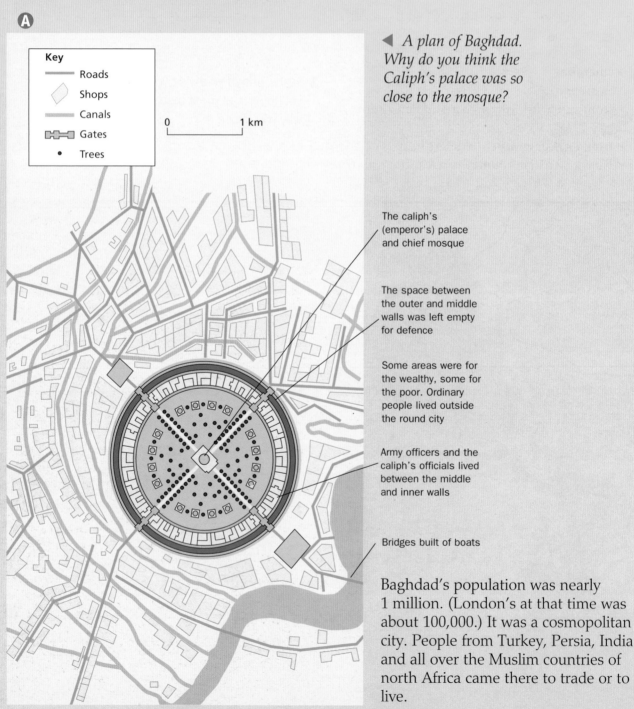

Key
- —— Roads
- ◇ Shops
- ═══ Canals
- ⊏⊐ Gates
- • Trees

0 ———— 1 km

◄ *A plan of Baghdad. Why do you think the Caliph's palace was so close to the mosque?*

The caliph's (emperor's) palace and chief mosque

The space between the outer and middle walls was left empty for defence

Some areas were for the wealthy, some for the poor. Ordinary people lived outside the round city

Army officers and the caliph's officials lived between the middle and inner walls

Bridges built of boats

Baghdad's population was nearly 1 million. (London's at that time was about 100,000.) It was a cosmopolitan city. People from Turkey, Persia, India and all over the Muslim countries of north Africa came there to trade or to live.

Homes and gardens

◀ Artist's impression of a rich family's house in Baghdad.

▼ A painting of a rich family relaxing in their garden, painted in the sixteenth century.

Houses in Baghdad were built of sun-dried bricks and the thick walls helped to keep the houses cool and secure. **Wealthy families** had carved wooden doors. Usually there were no windows on the outside: windows faced inside, onto the courtyard and garden where there were water fountains and orange and lemon trees. There were also covered walkways around the courtyard, where people could sit or walk out of the direct heat of the sun. Many houses also had an upper floor with a balcony. In some of the largest houses there were separate courtyards and rooms for female family members.

Poor families shared their homes with other families. Some built their own brick huts on the edges of the city. Others lived in closely packed brick houses without gardens. They would have very few windows to help keep them cool. The pathways between the houses were thin but shady and carefully laid out to tunnel wind through the streets and into the houses to help people keep cool.

In the streets and the markets

Baghdad was a trading city. Here are some of the things on sale in medieval times.

From India – wild animals such as tigers and elephants; leopard skins, rubies and coconuts.
From Arabia – horses, ostriches, camels and leather.
From China – silk, paper and ink, rhubarb, spices such as cinnamon and beautifully decorated porcelain.
From Egypt – donkeys (good for carrying, but not for riding), papyrus, jewels and oils.
From Turkey – silver and gold, beautiful cloth, slaves, marble, lyres and other musical instruments, horses.
From Russia – armour, helmets and slaves.

Pictures D–H show some medieval objects that you could have bought in Baghdad at that time. If you were a medieval visitor which of objects D–H would you most like to take home to England?

D *Pottery candlestick*

E *Necklace made of camel bone or wood*

F *A glass jug*

G *Lamps*

H *Carved wooden casket for storing valuables*

I *A row of shops in the bazaar: jeweller, herbalist, butcher and baker. What is happening in each shop?*

162

J *A slave market*

Slaves

Picture J shows a slave market. Rich people in Baghdad had slaves to do their work. Muslims were not allowed to own fellow Muslims as slaves so they imported slaves from Russia, Africa and other distant lands. The Islamic religion encouraged owners to take good care of slaves but we don't know how far they obeyed this teaching.

Entertainment

If you wanted entertainment rather than products you could listen to the storytellers in the street. Some of their stories are still well-known, including the tales of Aladdin and Ali Baba. There were also wine houses with dancers and musicians where men could go to relax.

K *A fabric shop and street scene. Can you find: a man being taken to court; a musician; a man buying cloth?*

The 'house of wisdom'

L *At the library*

One of the early rulers began the 'House of Wisdom' which included a vast library and a school. Translators were employed there to translate books from other languages into Arabic. Many of these books had been written by the Ancient Greeks and Romans but there were also books from India.

At the library, scholars studied mathematics, chemistry, astronomy and other sciences, including medicine. They knew far more about Greek and Roman ideas about medicine than the doctors in Europe did, especially before the 1300s.

There was also a hospital in Baghdad, which was built in 805. Doctors worked there full time and there were students learning to be doctors. There were even separate wards for different diseases and a pharmacy where medicines were mixed.

M *Illustration from a medieval book showing how to treat a leprosy patient.*

Mosques

Baghdad was full of mosques. Many were beautiful buildings, decorated with abstract patterns and designs. Each neighbourhood would have its own mosque.

Baghdad's Mosque al-Kazimayn. An engraving made in the nineteenth century. This mosque replaced a medieval mosque. There are no pictures of Baghdad's medieval mosques.

A prince leading Friday prayers.

Rats or rebels?
Which was more significant?

Welcome to Significance Alley! Over the next eighteen pages you are going to investigate in detail two important events – the Black Death and the Peasants' Revolt. They were both significant – because they both caused great changes in people's lives. Your big task will be to decide which of them had the **most** impact, and this is how you are going to do it... at Significance Alley.

How does Significance Alley work?
Each of the skittles represents a different aspect of people's lives. You are going to test the significance of each event – the Black Death and the Peasants' Revolt – by seeing how many of these skittles it knocks over.

ACTIVITY

Read about the two events below. Discuss:

1 How do you think each event will affect the lives of the people of England? Try to think of as many effects as possible for each event.
2 Which event do you think will turn out to be more significant when you have investigated them all? Keep a note of your prediction and look again at it when you revisit Significance Alley on pages 184–185.

The Black Death, 1348

The Black Death was a terrible disease that spread across Asia and Europe and reached England in 1348. It killed nearly half the population in a year and there were many more outbreaks of the disease in the next 300 years. We don't know for sure how the disease spread but the most likely explanation is that it was carried by rats.

The Peasants' Revolt, 1381

The revolt was a great rebellion around London and there were small revolts in other parts of the country too. The rebels took control of London, burned homes and murdered the Archbishop of Canterbury. The rebellion lasted several weeks before the King and the nobles could stop it.

The Black Death

What was the Black Death?

In 1348 a mystery disease started killing many people in England. They did not know what caused it. They called it simply the pestilence. But historians have worked out quite a lot about it. These two pages summarise what we know.

The causes

The Black Death was probably a disease called bubonic plague. Bubonic plague is carried by rats and passed from rat to rat by fleas. When a flea bites an infected rat it becomes infected itself and then passes the disease on to the next rat it bites. Infected fleas can also pass the disease on to humans. These fleas multiply quickly in warm weather but die off in cold weather so bubonic plague spreads more quickly in summer.

The Black Death was probably made worse by a second deadly disease at the same time called pneumonic plague. This attacks the lungs. This is not affected by weather or climate.

Of course the people of the Middle Ages did not know this. They did not understand the causes of disease because they did not know about germs.

The spread

The Black Death spread from Asia. In around 1345 people in China and India were dying. From there it spread steadily into Europe carried by rats and fleas along the trading routes. It probably arrived in England in summer 1348 on a boat from France. This is how one medieval writer records it:

> In June 1348, in Melcombe, in the county of Dorset, two ships came alongside. One of the sailors had brought with him from Gascony the seeds of the terrible pestilence and, through him, the men of that town were the first in England to be infected.

ACTIVITY

Create your own quiz using the information on these pages. Write at least five questions. Include at least one question for each of the four information boxes.

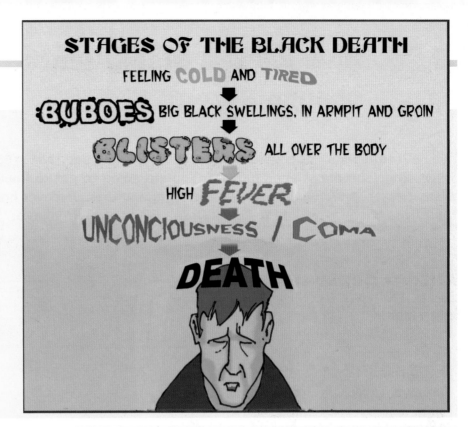

STAGES OF THE BLACK DEATH

FEELING COLD AND TIRED

⬇

BUBOES BIG BLACK SWELLINGS, IN ARMPIT AND GROIN

⬇

BLISTERS ALL OVER THE BODY

⬇

HIGH FEVER

⬇

UNCONCIOUSNESS / COMA

⬇

DEATH

The symptoms

After a person is bitten by a flea bubonic plague develops quickly. The first symptoms appear after just two or three days, and the victim usually dies between four to seven days later. Some lucky or strong people can survive bubonic plague but it kills most of those who catch it.

The victims

People in the Middle Ages were used to death and disease. But this disease was more deadly than any they had ever known. In Britain, at least 2 million people died in just one year. This was over 40 per cent of the population. In London the death rate was even worse. Probably half the population died – 50,000 people. Many millions more died in other countries in Europe and Asia.

It affected every part of society. It affected towns and villages. It killed both rich and poor people; adults and children.

SOURCE 1 *Burying the dead in London. Despite the horror and the number of deaths, the bodies were still laid carefully in graves.*

SOURCE 2 *A painting from a church in France showing a blindfolded Black Death killing rich and poor alike.*

How did the Black Death change Allton?

In 1347 Allton was a peaceful village. Here you can see the villagers celebrating a good harvest. You are going to get to know these people, find out their hopes and fears and then discover how their lives changed when the Black Death reached their village.

Allton, September 1347

REMEMBER

Villeins (V) were not free. They had to work for the lord and could not leave the village without his permission.

Freemen (F) could live and work wherever they liked.

The lord (Sir John Lovell) owned the land in the village. The villeins worked for him part of the week in return for the use of some land.

ACTIVITY

1 Which villagers are hopeful about the future?
2 Why are they hopeful?
3 Which villagers are not looking forward to the future?
4 Why are they pessimistic?
5 Who is doing well in 1347:
   a) the lord
   b) the villeins
   c) the freemen?

John Morell (F)
Of course! We'll get good prices for our crops with so many in the town wanting food.

Margery Morell (F)
Can we afford new ribbons for my hair?

Tom Dover (F)
I don't sell so many ribbons nowadays.

Henry Brewer (F)
Most freemen aren't as lucky as you, John. I've only got enough land to grow food for my family.

Roger Lincoln (F)
Try the lord and his family. They are the rich ones.

Joanna Brewer

Adam Morell

Alice Brewer (F)

Christina Baker

Baby Isabella

Mathilda Legg (V)

Agnes Baker (V)
Did you see the youngsters playing? So healthy! So happy!

John Baker (V)
It's a good time for Isabella to be born. With the good harvest there'll be plenty of food for us all through the winter.

John Newton (V)
Sir John says that we can leave the village after we're married next month. We'll find jobs in the town and make some money.

171

Allton, September 1349

Here is the same village two years later. The Black Death has wreaked havoc. Half of the villagers have died.

ACTIVITY

1 Compare this picture with the previous two pages. If someone is no longer in the picture, it means they have died. Can you list the people who have disappeared?

Now read the speech bubbles of the survivors on these two pages.

2 Which villagers are hopeful about the future?

3 Why are they hopeful?
4 Which villagers are not looking forward to the future?
5 Why are they pessimistic?
6 Who is doing well in 1349:
   a) the lord
   b) the villeins
   c) the freemen?

Henry Brewer (F)

I could do very well in the next few years, Margery. I can earn high wages by working on Sir Robert's lands, and use the money to buy land. You've got land to spare and no one to farm it. I'll give you a good price for your land – or you could think of marrying me.

Margery Morell (F)

No, thank you, Henry. Adam and I will manage, even if we have to sell a little land.

Richard Carter (V)

So much for the chance to go to school! I'm stuck as a shepherd because there's no one else to do it.

Adam Morell

Sir Robert Lovell

Where can we find more workers, Stephen? The crops are rotting in the fields and the animals are wandering free. My income is far less than my father's before the pestilence came.

Stephen Cakebread the Steward (F)

I don't know, my lord. We can offer higher wages but no one is looking for more work.

Lady Alice Lovell

I am glad your father did not free the villeins. They have to work for us and we don't have to pay them high wages.

172

173

'How I survived the Black Death!'

The Black Death devastated Allton. It killed half the people in the village. Other villages in England suffered just as badly.

Now you are going to tell the story of the Black Death from the perspective of one of the survivors in Allton.

ACTIVITY

Work with a partner and choose one of these four characters.

Sir Robert Lovell   **John Baker**   **Edith Smith**   **Margery Morell**

> Let me tell you my story.

You have to tell their story. We will give you advice on how to write your story.

- Use the information about the villagers on pages 170–173 and the background information on pages 168–169.
- You can tell it in the first person and you can use the story recipe below.
- Also, try to remember what you have found out about life in medieval villages. Put in some good detail.

STORY RECIPE

1 SCARY NEWS!
Write about how you first heard about the pestilence and how people reacted.

2 THE PESTILENCE ARRIVES!
Write about who became ill first and what were the symptoms.
Who was the first to die and how did they die?

3 DESPERATE REMEDIES!
Write about what you think caused the pestilence and how you tried to treat it.

4 THE AFTERMATH!
Write about what life in the village is like now.
What does the future hold for you?
Who is dead? Who has survived?

---

 1 SCARY NEWS!
Write about how you first heard about the pestilence and how people reacted.

Here are some of the stories passed on from village to village in 1348 that warned of the terrible disease even before it arrived. Choose one to include in your story. How would your character have heard and how would they have reacted?

> Did you hear about that ship that ran aground on the coast? Everyone aboard was dead – with awful blisters on their bodies.

> News from Willington – so many people are dying, there aren't enough people alive to bury the dead.

Starters

The first I heard was...

A visitor arrived who told me...

I was doing my household chores one day when...

2 THE PESTILENCE ARRIVES!

Write about who became ill first and what were the symptoms. Who was the first to die and how did they die?

Who became ill first? How did people react? Choose one of your character's friends or relatives in Allton (see pages 170–173) and explain what happened. The symptoms and stages of the disease are explained on page 169. How did your character feel when their friend or relative suffered or died? Did your character get ill and survive, or were they one of the lucky ones who didn't get ill at all?

SOURCE 1

An Irish monk, Brother John Clynn

I, waiting among the dead for death to come, leave parchment for continuing the work, in case anyone should still be alive in the future and any son of Adam can escape this pestilence and continue my work.

Starters

When the pestilence finally arrived, the first to fall ill was...

One Sunday morning at church I noticed Agnes shivering...

In the middle of the night I heard...

The first funeral was for...

We thought... was as good as dead, but one day...

We counted the coffins. There were...

3 DESPERATE REMEDIES!

Write about what you think caused the pestilence and how you tried to treat it.

People at the time didn't know what caused the Black Death so they didn't know how to treat it. But here are some explanations that people gave at the time.
- Which explanation would your character believe?
- What would he or she say about the other explanations?
- See page 176 for some of the remedies people tried. Which remedy would your character use to try to stop the pestilence spreading? Make sure their remedy matches their explanation.

Starters

Father William had the first idea. He suggested...

We blamed... so we...

It's a punishment from God because we have been **wicked**.

The air has been infected by evil **vapours** released by earthquakes. That's what is killing people.

It's the **planets**. Saturn, Jupiter and Mars are close together. That's always a sign of wonderful, terrible or violent things.

Explanations

It's all the fault of the children who do not obey their **parents**. That's why God is punishing us with this pestilence.

God is punishing us because of the ridiculous **fashions** people wear nowadays.

My doctor says that the plague is caused because the **humours** in people's bodies are out of balance.

They lit **fires** and spread **perfumes** in the air to keep away the bad smells.

They **prayed** to God for forgiveness for all their sins.

They **bled** the sick and **purged** them to empty their bowels. This was to balance their humours and so make them better!

Attempted remedies

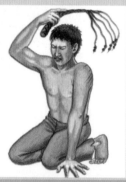

They **whipped** themselves until it really hurt so God knew they were sorry.

They made a **candle** as tall as a man, or even big enough to encircle a village, and burned it night and day.

SOURCE 2

Boccaccio, an Italian writer, wrote:

Some thought that by **living quietly** they could avoid the danger. Others said that plenty of drinking, singing and enjoyment would stop the plague. Day and night they went from one tavern to another, drinking and **running wild**.

The King ordered all the streets in the cities to be **cleaned** of rubbish and animal dung.

4 THE AFTERMATH!
Write about what life in the village is like now.
What does the future hold for you?
Who is dead? Who has survived?

One year later. The pestilence is over. What is life like in the village now?
Use the conversations on pages 170–173 to help you.
• What has happened to the people of Allton?
• Who has died? Who has survived?
• Are the survivors better off, or worse off?
• Physically, what has changed?

Think about thoughts and feelings too.
• How has the Black Death affected people's attitudes?
• What do they hope for in the future?

Starters

Life will never be the same again because...

My saddest memory is...

Woe is me! My friends and family are...

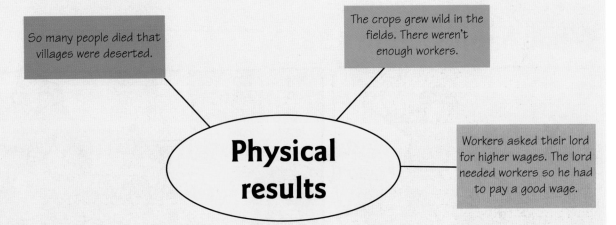

So many people died that villages were deserted.

The crops grew wild in the fields. There weren't enough workers.

Physical results

Workers asked their lord for higher wages. The lord needed workers so he had to pay a good wage.

SOURCE 3

An Italian writer, Petrarch, wrote this in a letter to a friend in 1350

Where are our dear friends? Where are the beloved faces, the relaxed and enjoyable conversations? There was a crowd of friends. Now I am almost alone. I should make new friends but how, when the human race is almost wiped out, and why, when it looks as if the end of the world is at hand?

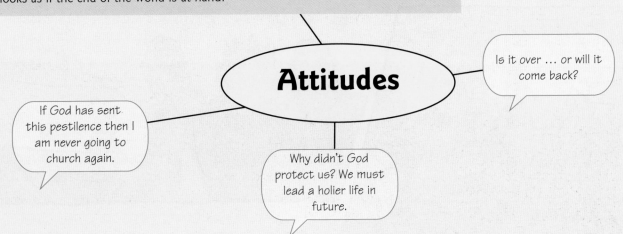

Attitudes

Is it over ... or will it come back?

If God has sent this pestilence then I am never going to church again.

Why didn't God protect us? We must lead a holier life in future.

The Peasants' Revolt

Were the rebels of 1381 heroes or villains?

The Black Death wasn't the only great event to affect the people of Allton. Just over 30 years later, in 1381, the villagers joined a great revolt and marched on London. Some people treat these rebels as heroes. Others see them as villains. What will you decide?

ACTIVITY 1

1 Read the story strip of the revolt.
   a) What do you think attracted villagers to join in?
   b) What do you think worried their lords?
2 Look back to the words of Sir Robert and Lady Alice on page 172. Can you see a link between the Black Death and the Peasants' Revolt?

What happened in 1381?

1 In May, villagers in Essex refused to pay taxes and attacked the tax collectors. They quickly won support from other villages in Kent and Essex.

2 7 June. The rebels freed a priest called John Ball from prison in Kent. Ball had been imprisoned for saying that all men should be equal and free.

3 12 June. The rebels arrived at Blackheath near London. Their leader was Wat Tyler.

4 13 June. King Richard, who was only fourteen, went by river to meet the rebels. But there was so much confusion he did not land and there was no meeting.

The rebels entered London and burned down the Duke of Lancaster's house.

14 June. The King talked to the rebels and agreed that all villeins should be freemen and all rebels would be pardoned. Meanwhile, some rebels attacked the Tower of London and murdered the Archbishop of Canterbury and other advisers of the King.

15 June. The King met the rebels' leader, Wat Tyler, at Smithfield and Tyler was killed by one of the King's men. The King ordered the rebels to go home, repeating the promise that they would all become freemen. They went home.

ACTIVITY 2

Now you know the main parts of the story you are going to read the evidence of Thomas of Walsingham. Thomas was a monk at the monastery of St Albans, north-west of London. He was an intelligent man who described the rebellion in detail.

3 Do you expect Thomas to write an unbiased, objective account of the revolt? Give at least one reason for your prediction.

4 Do you expect Thomas to treat the rebels as heroes or villains? Give at least one reason for your prediction.

Thomas of Walsingham's History of the Peasants' Revolt

1 At this time England suffered a dreadful calamity. If God had not put an end to it, the whole kingdom would have been destroyed. The villeins and other peasants in Essex, in their stupidity, demanded their freedom, planning to take control of all things and be the equal of their lords. Men from the villages where this started sent messengers telling everyone to join them. Anyone who refused would have their homes burned and their heads cut from their necks. In a short time 5000 of the poorest peasants assembled. They wanted to conquer the kingdom but some had only sticks, some swords covered in rust, some only axes and some had arrows with only one feather. Only one in a thousand of the rascals was properly armed.

[Thomas says that, by the time the rebels arrived near London, their army had swollen to 100,000.]

2 The Mayor of London ordered the city gates to be closed but the common people of the city supported the peasants and threatened to kill the Mayor if the gates were closed. And so the rogues got into the city. They said they only wanted to punish the traitors to the King, especially the Duke of Lancaster, and there would be no robberies.

3 But later that day, when the rebels had been drinking heavily, they burned down the Duke of Lancaster's house. Then they burned more houses and attacked the Tower of London where the King and his advisers were staying. In their madness, they demanded the King hand over Archbishop Sudbury and others whom they called traitors. The King agreed, knowing he would be killed if he did not agree. There were 600 soldiers in the Tower but they did nothing to stop the rebels.

4 When the ruffians got into the Tower they arrogantly sat joking on the King's bed and several asked the King's mother for a kiss. They were the lowest kinds of peasant but they behaved like lords. Swineherds thought themselves better than knights. Then these devils found the Archbishop, dragged him outside and hacked off his head. They executed many others as if it was a game.

5 Then the King offered Walter Tyler, the rebels' leader, a pardon if they stopped the killing, burning and robberies. Tyler said he would accept the pardon provided that the King agreed to all his demands. Above all he wanted to execute all lawyers and have no laws because then the common people would decide everything.

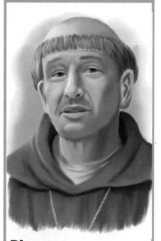

ACTIVITY 3

Discuss:
Heroes or villains?

5 Read paragraph 1. What do the blue highlighted phrases tell you about Thomas' attitude to the rebels?

6 Which other details does Thomas include in paragraph 1 to back up his view of the rebels?

7 Read the green highlighted phrases. What words would you use to describe the rebels after reading these phrases?

8 Read the yellow highlighted phrases. According to Thomas, what did the rebels want?

6 Tyler met the King at Smithfield. The meeting began with a quarrel when Sir John Newton, one of the King's knights, rode to meet Tyler. Tyler was so arrogant that he thought Newton should be on foot. The two men threatened each other with knives until the King ordered Newton to put down his knife and climb down from his horse. The King wanted to calm the rascal Tyler but the scoundrel attacked Newton in front of the King. Then the Mayor of London, and other knights loyally raced forward to help Newton. The King ordered them to arrest Tyler. The Mayor, a man of great bravery, struck Tyler on the head and others attacked him with their swords. Tyler fell from his horse, dead.

7 Immediately the rebels shouted 'Our captain is dead. He has been treacherously killed' and they drew their bows ready to fire on the King and his men. But the King, with great courage for so young a man, spurred his horse towards the common people and said 'Surely you do not want to fire upon me, your King? Follow me and you can have all that you have asked for.'

8 Meanwhile, the Mayor of London gathered a small army of loyal men and they rode to help the King. They surrounded the peasants. Throwing down their axes, bows and spears, the rebels humbly sank to their knees and asked for mercy. To stop trouble the King ordered that they be given the charter they had asked for. The charter said that the King gave everyone their freedom. They were also pardoned for taking part in the rebellion.

9 Once they had the charter they all returned home. Once the kingdom was peaceful, John Straw and the other leaders who had been arrested were executed and later the Charter of Freedom and Pardon was revoked.

ⓘ At the same time as this revolt in London there was another rebellion in St Albans, where Thomas was a monk. The rebels in St Albans wanted more freedom from the monastery, which owned a lot of the local land. Thomas thought they were wrong because he believed that God decided which men were free and which weren't and so he thought the rebels were challenging God.

ACTIVITY 4

Digging deeper

9 Read paragraph 4 and the information on page 179 about Thomas. How do they help to explain Thomas' attitude to the revolt?

10 Read the whole of Thomas' History or ask your teacher to play a recording of it. Choose two more details that you think best sum up Thomas's attitude to the rebels.

11 Do you think Thomas has written a fair and accurate account of the rebellion? Think about:
- is he fair to both sides?
- how do you think he found out exactly what happened?

Heroes or villains?

12 Now you have read Thomas' History what do you think of the rebels? Would you describe them as heroes or villains? Give some evidence from the last four pages to back up your choice.

181

Was Thomas a good historian?

Thomas' account is full of lots of useful and interesting details but it is obviously biased against the rebels. When historians are faced with a one-sided source they compare it with other sources to see if they agree. That is what you are going to do now.

Sadly, none of the rebels wrote their story or, if they did, it was destroyed long ago. But historians have found out a lot more about the rebels, using records from law courts and Parliament, and tax records. You are going to look at three topics and check whether Thomas was right. Was he a good historian?

Topic 1: Why did the revolt begin?

Thomas said:

They wanted to… conquer the kingdom… take control of all things… to be free.

ℹ WHAT THE OTHER SOURCES TELL US

People had been angry with the government for 30 years! After the Black Death the survivors thought that, as there weren't enough workers, they would be able to earn more money and move around to get better jobs. But King Edward III said 'No!'

He made a law (the Statute of Labourers) that said everyone had to work in the same villages and for the same wages as before the Black Death. And villeins could not be set free. People hated this law but they did not dare rebel against the lords.

Then the French attacked and burned English towns. The new king, Richard II, was only ten so everyone blamed his uncle, the Duke of Lancaster, who should have led the lords to stop the French. Then Lancaster made things even worse. He collected a Poll Tax. 'Poll' means 'head'. The idea was that every 'head' or person paid the same, whether a poor person or a duke.

This tax was seen as very unfair so, in 1380, many people hid when the tax collectors came to their villages. In Essex, for example, 48,000 people had paid the Poll Tax in 1377 but in 1380 only 30,000 people paid. They did not rebel, they hid!

It was when they heard that the tax collectors were coming back, with orders to find everyone who had hidden and punish them that the rebellion actually started. Hiding wouldn't work this time.

ACTIVITY 1

1 According to the other sources what were the three reasons why people were angry before 1381?
2 What did people do to avoid paying the tax in 1380?
3 What development triggered the rebellion?
4 Do you agree or disagree with Thomas' explanation of what the rebels wanted? Give at least one reason for your choice.

Thomas said they were:

> ruffians...
> the poorest peasants...
> stupid... only one in a thousand was properly armed

ⓘ WHAT THE OTHER SOURCES TELL US

Records show that many rebels were the leading men and women in their villages. They included constables and reeves, who organised the farmworkers.

Some rebels were leaders of the local forces who had been trained to fight off French attacks. They had horses, good weapons and plans for organising themselves quickly.

ACTIVITY 2

5 Which of these pictures A or B better illustrates Thomas' description of the rebels? Explain your choice.

6 Look at the box above. Which picture, A or B, best fits this evidence? Explain why.

7 a) What ideas come into your head when you hear the word 'peasant'?

b) Would you call this revolt the Peasants' Revolt (which used to be the common name) or the Great Revolt (which is used more nowadays)? Explain the reasons for your choice.

Topic 3: Did the rebellion suceed?

Thomas said:

> ...the leaders were executed and the Charter of Freedom and Pardon was revoked.

ⓘ WHAT THE OTHER SOURCES TELL US

Thomas was right about the end of the revolt. However, that was not the end of the story. Many landowners were frightened by the revolt. They freed the villeins to avoid more rebellions. By 1450 all workers were free. They could work wherever they liked and earn higher wages.

ACTIVITY 3

Thomas clearly thought the rebels were villains. How far do you agree with him? Where would you put the rebels of 1381 on this scale:

0   1   2   3   4   5

Villains   Heroes

8 Write some sentences giving evidence to back up your score.

Welcome back to Significance Alley!

Now you know about Rats and Rebels it's time to decide which one had the most impact. So pick up your bowling shoes and take your place in Significance Alley!

ACTIVITY

Take each impact ball from page 185 in turn.

1 Decide which skittle it is aiming at.

2 **Two** of the skittles have been missed completely because the Black Death and the Peasants' Revolt did not affect them. Which skittles are they?

3 **Three** skittles were hit by the Black Death ball but not by the Peasants' Revolt ball.

   a) Which skittles were they?

   b) Award the Black Death 3 points if it knocked the skittle over completely (had a huge effect on the skittle); 2 points if it made the skittle totter (had some effect on the skittle); 1 point if it just touched the skittle (had hardly any effect on the skittle).

4 Now there are **five** skittles left. They were hit by both the Black Death and the Peasants' Revolt balls. Take each skittle in turn. You have 3 points to award for each skittle. Divide the 3 points between the Black Death and the Peasants' Revolt balls according to which hit the skittle the hardest. For example, if the Black Death had a bigger effect than the Peasants' Revolt give the Black Death 2 points and the Peasants' Revolt 1 point.

5 Add up the points won by the Black Death and by the Peasants' Revolt. Have the Rats or the Rebels won the Significance contest?

6 Think about the winning event. Why was it more significant than the other event?

7 Look back at your prediction on page 167. Was your prediction correct?

A

The **Black Death** interrupted the war between England and France and they were at peace. However Edward III invaded France again in 1355 and won a great victory at Poitiers.

B

There were no breakthroughs in medicine despite all the deaths. Doctors still did not understand what caused disease.

C

Half the people in Britain died from the **Black Death**. More died in later outbreaks of the disease. It took over 300 years for the population to recover to the same as before the Black Death.

D

The **Black Death** led to some freemen earning higher wages but the government tried to stop wages rising. However the **Peasants' Revolt** showed that the government could not stop people wanting to earn more. After this, wages gradually increased because there were not enough workers and so lords had to pay higher wages to get people to work for them.

F

People spent their increased wages on clothes (they had more colourful clothes), food (they ate more meat and a more varied diet) and on rebuilding their homes.

E

After the **Black Death** people began to demand their freedom but the lords refused. This led to the **Peasants' Revolt** in 1381. It failed but frightened lords into setting the villeins free. By the mid-1400s everyone was free.

I

Praying to God had not protected people from the **Black Death** so some people began to criticise the bishops and priests. However this had little impact.

G

People did the same kinds of work as they had before. Most people worked as farmers.

H

Some people spent their higher wages on sending their sons to school. The number of people who could read and write began to increase quickly. This began after the **Black Death** but increased after the **Peasants' Revolt**.

J

Most kinds of fun stayed the same – singing, dancing, sports and storytelling. More people went to school, learned to read and so enjoyed reading stories like the tales of King Arthur or Robin Hood. This happened in the 1400s thanks to the combined effects of the **Black Death** and the **Peasants' Revolt**.

History is a big subject. You can study anything that happened at any time in the past, to anybody, anywhere! You will never run out of material. So how does anyone decide what to study? That's easy – you just study the significant bits! But here's a problem: not everyone agrees about what is significant. So this Doing History is all about significance and how people decide who or what is significant.

> **Significance**
>
> People use different criteria to decide what is significant and this leads to debates and arguments

What was our criterion?

We decided to include depth studies of the Black Death and the Peasants' Revolt in this book because we think they are very significant events. The criterion we used to say they were significant was:

They changed people's lives!

and the skittles represent the aspects of life we considered. The more aspects of life were affected, the more significant we said it was.

1. Discuss which event, the Black Death or the Peasants' Revolt, knocked over more skittles.
2. Did you all agree on which event was more significant?

> **What does criteria mean?**
>
> The word 'criteria' means reasons for a choice. For example, one of your reasons to choose a holiday may be that it will be sunny. If so 'somewhere sunny' is your criterion for a good holiday! (Criterion is the singular of criteria.)

What other criteria do people use?

Impact on people's lives is not the only possible criterion we could use. In fact there are many different possible criteria.

Here are some people speaking about the significance of the Black Death and Peasants' Revolt. What criteria are they using to decide significance?

> **1** The Black Death affected many countries but the Peasants' Revolt affected only Britain. That must make the Black Death more significant than the Peasants' Revolt.

> **3** Thomas of Walsingham thought that the whole kingdom would be destroyed by the Peasants' Revolt. It was very significant to him.

> **2** The work we did on the Black Death was much more interesting than the work we did on the Peasants' Revolt so I suggest we get rid of the Peasants' Revolt in next year's course and study only the Black Death.

> **4** The Black Death is a bit like AIDS today as it sweeps around the world. So surely the way people reacted then has something to teach us today – that's the reason we study history, isn't it?

LEARNING LOG

You will do more work on significance later in the course and you will try out some other criteria for judging significance. How will you record what you have learned about criteria so you can remember it and use it next time?

① What criterion is each speaker using?
② Can you think of any other reasons why the Peasants' Revolt or the Black Death is, or is not, significant?

THE BIG STORY: Ordinary Life Part Two

In Sections 4 and 5 you have studied ordinary, everyday life across 400 years. Through Key Stage 3 you're going to follow life across 1000 years – and here it is in one diagram! Can you spot the key reasons why life improved – and got worse?

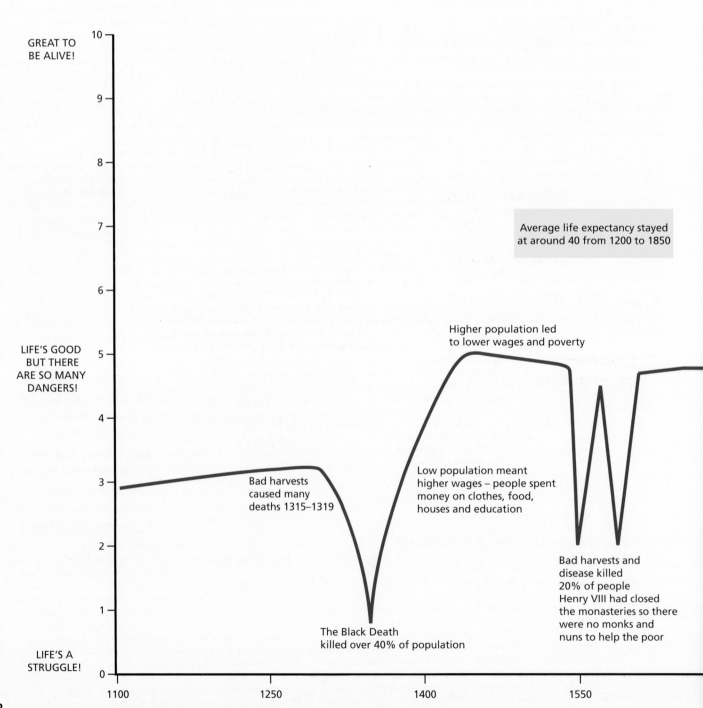

GREAT TO BE ALIVE!

LIFE'S GOOD BUT THERE ARE SO MANY DANGERS!

LIFE'S A STRUGGLE!

Average life expectancy stayed at around 40 from 1200 to 1850

Higher population led to lower wages and poverty

Low population meant higher wages – people spent money on clothes, food, houses and education

Bad harvests caused many deaths 1315–1319

The Black Death killed over 40% of population

Bad harvests and disease killed 20% of people Henry VIII had closed the monasteries so there were no monks and nuns to help the poor

1100   1250   1400   1550

ACTIVITY

Study the graph carefully.

1 Find two periods when there were big improvements in everyday life.

2 Find two periods when everyday life got worse.

3 Read the labels which explain why these changes happened. List as many different reasons as you can.

4 Do you think this graph shows what life was like for everybody? (Remember what you studied on pages 42–43.)

5 What most surprises you or interests you about this graph? Explain your choice.

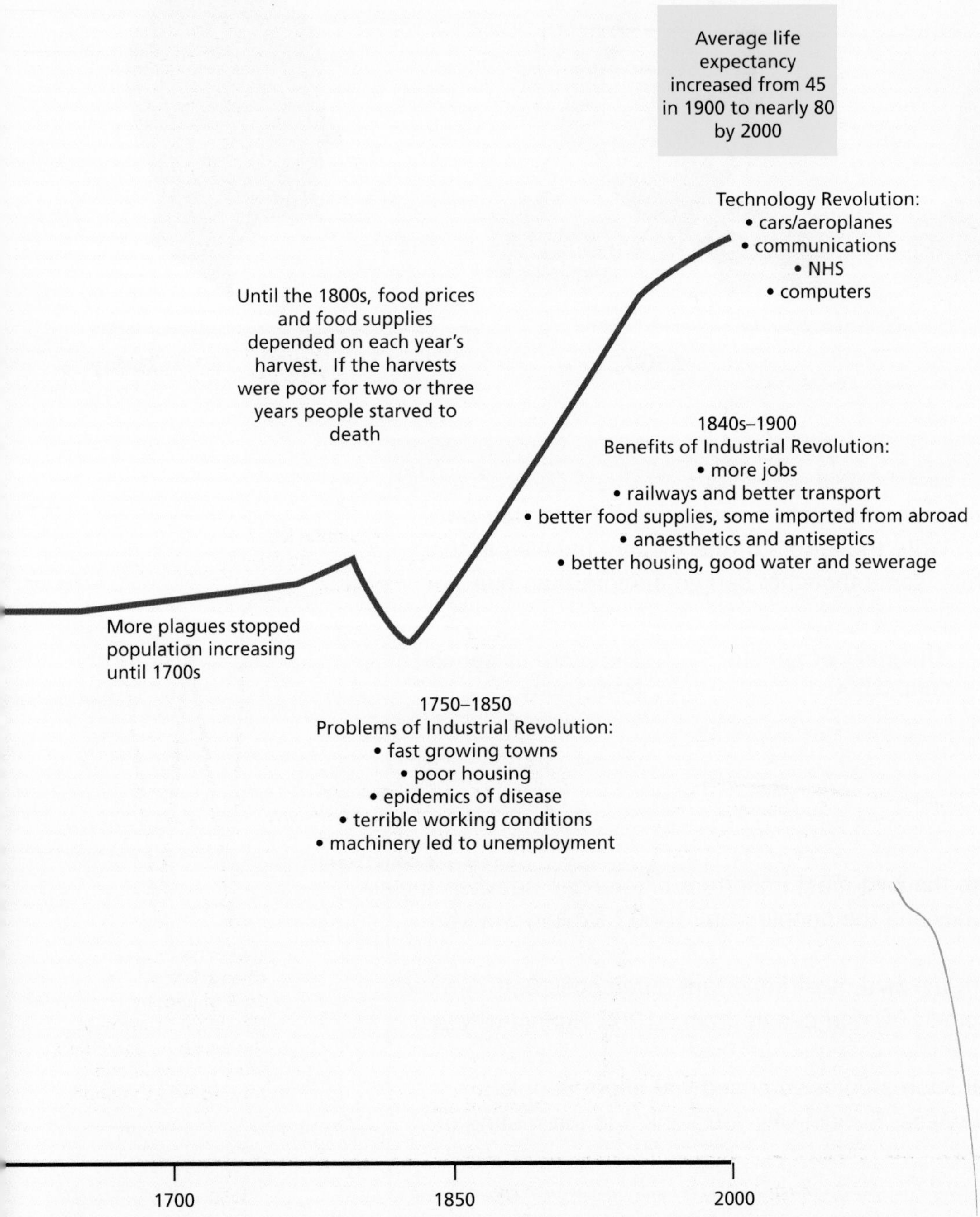

Average life expectancy increased from 45 in 1900 to nearly 80 by 2000

Technology Revolution:
- cars/aeroplanes
- communications
- NHS
- computers

Until the 1800s, food prices and food supplies depended on each year's harvest. If the harvests were poor for two or three years people starved to death

1840s–1900
Benefits of Industrial Revolution:
- more jobs
- railways and better transport
- better food supplies, some imported from abroad
- anaesthetics and antiseptics
- better housing, good water and sewerage

More plagues stopped population increasing until 1700s

1750–1850
Problems of Industrial Revolution:
- fast growing towns
- poor housing
- epidemics of disease
- terrible working conditions
- machinery led to unemployment

1700   1850   2000

Into the mind of a medieval villager!

The people below lived hundreds of years apart. Two of them lived in the Middle Ages – in 1100 (just after the Norman Conquest) and in 1500 (just before Henry VIII became king). The other one could be you, someone who is alive today. They lived in different kinds of homes, wore different clothes, did different things for fun – but were their ideas and thoughts different too?

1100   1500   today

ACTIVITY

1 Who was thinking each of the thoughts on page 191? Fill in your own copy of a grid like this. Write the letters of the thought bubbles in the columns but be careful – some thoughts can go in more than one column!

Thoughts of people from 1100	Thoughts of people from 1500	Thoughts of people from today

2 Which do you think are the **two** most important differences between the thoughts of people today and the people from 1500? Explain why you chose them.

3 Which do you think are the **two** most important differences between the thoughts of people from 1500 and people from 1100? Explain why you chose them.

4 Choose one thing that interested or surprised you about people's thoughts in the Middle Ages. Explain why you think it is interesting or surprising.

A Only another week and we can get the harvest in. We must pray it doesn't pour with rain now and ruin the crops. If we have another bad harvest many people will go hungry this winter. Some poor folk may even starve to death if it's really bad.

B These Norman lords have caused so much fear and worry. Nobody understands what they're saying. They could be joking or they could be planning to take away our homes and animals.

C Thanks be to God for the good monks at the monastery. If there is no work, or food prices are high, we can depend on the monks to give us help.

D I've heard my grandfather tell what it was like in the olden days. He says half the villagers weren't free to leave the village. They had to work on the lord's land two or even three days a week. I'm glad all that's changed and now everyone's free.

E My grandfather says we youngsters don't know how well off we are. He reckons we've got more money to spend than when he was young. He wanted to go to school but there was no money so he had to work in the fields like everyone else.

F I'd better be careful using this saw. Poor old John cut his finger doing this and it went bad and he was dead within the week.

G My sister's got terrible toothache. It's been really bad all week. She's used honey and tried a herbal remedy our mother gave her but nothing's doing any good.

H I wonder what it's like being old? There's someone in our village who reckons he's over sixty. Not many live to be that old.

I My two weeks of holiday are coming up soon. I'm off to the seaside for some sunshine.

J My wife's been off work sick for three months. I don't know what we'd have done without her sick pay or if we'd had to pay for her to be in hospital.

K It's back-breaking work bringing the harvest in but at least there's plenty of holidays coming up. It's a good time of year for celebrating saints' days.

L If we put in some extra hours at work we'll go into town to buy those new clothes. And I reckon next year we'll be able to afford to make big improvements to the house too.

M I've done well and live far more comfortably than my father but with luck and hard work my sons will do even better. I've got high hopes for them.

You are now going to study a period known as the Renaissance (the 'rebirth') when there were many new ideas appearing in Europe. Old medieval attitudes were being questioned by some people, and new modern ideas were being developed which changed important parts of people's lives.

In this short section you find out about those new ideas, how they spread, which of them caused the most excitement and why! Finally, you will look into the mind of an English king (Henry VIII, the most famous English king) who ruled at the end of this period and decide 'were Henry's ideas medieval or modern?'

So, what's new?

Welcome to our Renaissance Gallery. All these people are famous for their achievements or their new ideas. Hear what they have to say about their new ideas.

GROUP 1: EXPLORERS

MAGELLAN (1480–1521)

COLUMBUS (1451–1500)

VASCO DA GAMA (1460–1524)

We developed better, stronger ships and better compasses so we sailors could travel further. I tried to sail all the way round the world. I was the first European explorer to sail into the Pacific. I wanted to bring home spices and luxuries to make me rich.

I wanted to explore the world. I sailed across the Atlantic Ocean. I was looking for a quicker way to get to India and China but I discovered a new continent (although I did not know it at the time! I thought I had found a new way to an old one!). I took Spanish people to settle there. I made new maps to show other ships how to get there.

Read the word bubbles from these Renaissance men on pages 192–195.

1 Choose one of these groups:
- explorers
- scientists
- artists

and write a sentence to sum up one of their 'new ideas'. For example a sentence about explorers might begin 'Europeans were looking for a quicker route around the world and...'

2 Look at group 4 on page 195. What was the one new 'idea' that helped spread the other new ideas?

3 Some of these ideas led to people being tortured or executed. Which of these new ideas do you think might cause the most serious arguments?

Paintings used to look flat and unrealistic. But I was a good observer and a skilled artist so my art looked very lifelike. Many people wanted me to paint for them – but my greatest triumph was to cover the whole ceiling of the Sistine chapel with paintings of Christian stories. It took years.

MICHELANGELO (1475–1564)

BOTTICELLI (1444–1510)

Instead of just painting religious art like painters used to I also painted pictures of ancient Greek myths like *The Birth of Venus*. Some of my paintings were burned because the Church said they were pagan.

GROUP 2: ARTISTS

DONATELLO (1386–1466)

I was an artist but I wanted to have a go at everything else too! I designed war machines, flying machines, canals, water pumps. Yet I also found time to paint the most famous picture in history – the *Mona Lisa*.

LEONARDO (1452–1519)

193

People used to say that the Sun orbits the Earth. I studied the skies carefully and from the movements of the planets I said for certain that was not the case. The Earth and all the other planets go round the Sun. Earth is not the centre of the universe. The Sun is!

With my improved telescope I proved that Copernicus was right about the Sun. I also did other science experiments – it's important to find things out for yourself, not just to believe what people tell you. But it got me into trouble. My books were banned by the Pope but he could not stop the ideas spreading.

People used to say that it was wrong to dissect dead bodies – they would be needed for the next life. But I dissected dead bodies to find out for myself how the muscles, bones and organs connect to each other. I made detailed drawings which were published as a book so any doctor or surgeon could see inside a body without cutting it up for themselves.

**COPERNICUS
(1473–1543)**

**GALILEO
(1564–1642)**

**VESALIUS
(1514–1564)**

Most of the characters have their own
websites. For example, find out more at The
Galileo Project (http://galileo.rice.edu) or
michelangelo.com.

Biographies and pictures can also be found
on www.wikipedia.org.

All books used to
be written out by hand.
But I brought the first
printing press to Europe.
Once we could make books
by the thousand all the
other new ideas spread
much more quickly than
before.

I carefully observed
what made a successful ruler
and I wrote a book of advice for
kings and princes on how to
keep and use power. I said they
had to be strong and ruthless
but they had to be fair.

I was a monk, then I
became a protester. I hated the
way the Catholic Church
distorted the truth of
Christianity. I wrote books
explaining what the Bible really
said. The Pope ordered them to
be burned.

**MACHIAVELLI
(1469–1527)**

**GUTENBERG
1400–1468**

**LUTHER
(1483–1546)**

Why did people argue so much about new religious ideas?

You already know how important religion was in the Middle Ages: very! So it won't surprise you that it was the new ideas about religion that caused the most argument. Here's why.

For over 1000 years almost all people in Western Europe had been Catholics. Then in the 1500s things began to change. There was a choice. The Catholic way or the Protestant way.

The Catholic way

On one side were people who believed the Catholic traditions had always been, and would remain, the way to get to heaven.

THE CATHOLIC WAY

1 Church services should be in Latin as they have been for 1000 years. It's familiar and it feeds people's faith.

2 People need priests to help them find God. The priest is the link between people and God. Priests should wear special robes to show this special status.

3 The bishops should appoint the priests. They know what's best.

4 The Bible is too hard for ordinary people to understand. They should be guided by the Pope. He is God's representative on Earth. He will tell them what God wants them to do.

5 Churches should be full of colour and fine statues of the saints. This decoration shows the glory of God.

6 What you believe is very important. If you believe the wrong thing you will go to hell for eternity.

The Protestant way

On the other side were people like Martin Luther who believed that the Catholic Church had lost its way. Luther was particularly cross about the way people could pay to have their sins forgiven, but this was only one criticism. In fact he wanted to reform the whole of Christianity so that it followed what the Bible said instead of what the Pope and the bishops said.

- Luther and his supporters were called **Protestants** because they were **protest**ing against the way the church was run.
- These changes are known as **The Reformation** because the Protestants wanted to **reform** Christianity.

Heretics

The Catholics believed that Protestant ideas were wrong. They believed that Protestants were 'heretics' who would go to hell. And that the people who spread these ideas were dangerous. Catholics believed they had a duty to stop Protestants spreading their false ideas – if necessary by executing them.

THE PROTESTANT WAY

A People should choose their own priests. They don't need bishops to choose them.

B Church services should be in English. Ordinary people do not understand Latin.

C Christians should be guided by the Bible not by the Pope. It is the word of God. The Bible should be translated into English then ordinary people can read it.

D What you believe is very important. If you believe the wrong thing you will go to hell for eternity.

E People don't need a priest or the Pope as a way to God. Jesus Christ and the Bible are the way to God.

F Churches should be simple and plain. Decoration draws attention away from God. We should get rid of statues and pictures in churches. And priests are not special people. They should wear simple clothes.

PROTESTANT

ACTIVITY

Discuss:

1 Compare the Catholic beliefs 1–6 and Protestant beliefs A–F. How do they disagree about:
   - Church decoration
   - The Pope
   - Priests
   - The Bible?

2 Is there anything that Catholics and Protestants agree about?

3 Which of the Protestant reforms do you think would have most impact on ordinary people in churches in English villages?

William Caxton, the man who ...

One of the developments that made these religious changes more controversial was printing. Through the Middle Ages books had to be copied by hand. This was slow and expensive. The printing press changed that and William Caxton was the man who ... well your task is to complete that sentence your own way.

The Story of William Caxton

When William Caxton was young, the most famous man in London was Sir Richard (Dick) Whittington. He was Lord Mayor four times and was very rich from buying and selling wool and cloth.

William wanted to be rich like Dick Whittington. He started to work for a London merchant who bought and sold wool and cloth.

William was clever and soon had his own cloth business. He moved abroad, to Bruges, the centre of the European cloth trade.

While in Europe, William got interested in a new business idea – printing books. In the 1450s, Johannes Gutenberg had developed the first printing press, in Germany. It was very successful. Many people wanted to buy books.

William went to Germany to find out more. He visited a printing press. He saw this was a good way to make money. There was a real demand for books. More people were learning to read in the 1400s. Printing produced lots of books more quickly than ever before.

1 Read the story of William Caxton. Here are some possible secrets of success. Which ones apply to Caxton? Look for evidence in the story.
- He knew what people wanted.
- He had friends in high places who helped him get started.
- He was always on the look out for new ideas.
- He was a skilled inventor.
- He was good at seeing the potential of other people's inventions.
- He wanted to get rich.
- He was lucky.

2 Complete this headline: 'Caxton, the man who …'

3 Write another 50 words explaining why Caxton should still be remembered today.

In 1473, William printed his first book in English. It was one of his favourite stories – the story of the Trojan War.

Then he bought his own press, returned to London and set up in business next to Westminster Abbey. It was the first printing press in England and this was his first book – The Canterbury Tales by Geoffrey Chaucer, printed in 1476.

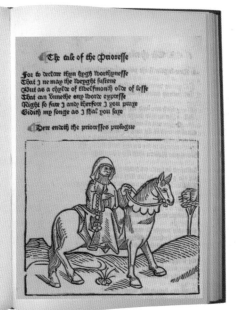

▼ SOURCE 1 *A stained glass window showing Caxton meeting Edward IV.*

The first printed books looked just like handwritten books. The letters were designed to look handwritten because people preferred this style. William didn't want his books to look cheap so he used this style.

William was a great success. He printed many books and became rich. He was invited to meet the king, Edward IV, and presented him with a book.

How did printing change ideas?

Printing is one of the most important inventions in history. It was a revolution which was as important in its time as the invention of the internet was in the late twentieth century. Here's why.

The printing revolution

BEFORE PRINTING
Books were copied by hand by **scriveners**. Twenty or more men worked in a room, writing out a story dictated to them by the **bookseller**. When they had finished writing out the story, the pages were sewn together and the bookseller had twenty or more copies to sell.
So ... there were not many books and hardly anyone could afford them.
So ... not many people learned to read.
So ... new ideas spread slowly.

AFTER PRINTING
Books could be printed quickly – hundreds at a time – which made them much cheaper. 
So ... there were far more and books and more people could afford them.
So ... more people learned to read.
So ... new ideas spread more quickly. In the early days of printing there were books about dozens of subjects such as history, travel, war and medicine as well as books of poems and stories. But the favourite subject for books was **religion** and the bestselling book of all was the Bible.

Why did printing cause arguments?

You can probably see why printing might worry some people:

- Political leaders did not want anyone to print materials that criticised them.
- Religious leaders were even more worried. They had been used to controlling people's beliefs. There had been new religious ideas before – but until printing they did not spread quickly. But now anyone could produce a book and the ideas might spread like wildfire.

What could they do? They tried three strategies:

Ban it!

For example, the Catholic Church ordered that Luther's books should be burned, and made a list of other books that Roman Catholics should not read.

Control it!

For example, in England printers had to get permission from the monarch for each book title they printed.

Use it!

For example, King Henry VIII ordered that a picture showing him at the centre of 'the great chain of being' be put in the front of all the Bibles printed in 1539. See Source 3.

▼ **SOURCE 1** *An illustration from Vesalius'* book The Fabric of the Human Body, *published in 1533.*

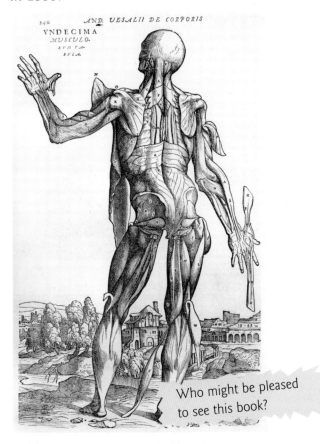

Who might be pleased to see this book?

▼ **SOURCE 2** *An illustration from a book published in the sixteenth century. The Pope is shown as a donkey.*

a) What is the message of this picture?
b) Who do you think might have created it?
c) Who do you think would oppose it?

◄ **SOURCE 3** *The opening page of the Bible in English printed in 1539. At the top of the page in the centre is King Henry VIII getting his instructions from God, passing them on to priests who then pass them on to the people who are all saying in Latin, 'Long live the King'.*

Why might Henry VIII be pleased about this picture?

ACTIVITY

1. List two reasons why printing helped ideas spread more quickly.
2. How is the development of printing similar to the development of the internet? List as many similarities as you can.

Why did people disagree about monasteries?

There were hundreds of monasteries in England. They had been an important part of religious life for centuries. Some of them were very rich because people gave them a lot of money. Many played a very practical part in people's lives, but in the early sixteenth century they were facing problems. Find out why.

My name is William Thornton. Welcome to St. Mary's Abbey in York. I am the abbot, in charge of the abbey and all our lands in Yorkshire and many other counties.

ACTIVITY

Study the information around the picture below.

1 Make a list of reasons why the monasteries were important to the people of York.
2 Which of the people mentioned do you think would suffer most if St Mary's Abbey was suddenly closed. Choose two and explain why you chose them and how life would change for them.

All the monks took a vow when they joined the monastery that they would live a very ordered life – devoted to serving God. They would pray five times a day, work hard the rest of the time, and not eat much. They were not supposed to marry because they were special people set apart to serve God. They were supposed to help the poor.

Brother Matthew has been here nearly all his life. Many of the 50 monks are elderly. They do not know any other way of life. Brother Matthew's job is to copy out old manuscripts for our library.

David is one of the 50 schoolboys who is educated at the abbey school free of charge. Monastery schools are the main way of providing education.

202

Brother Richard takes medicines, food and clothes to the sick in the city.

John, a stonemason, works with **Peter**, a glazier, to repair the abbey buildings. With so many buildings to look after there is always plenty of work for builders.

Old Meg is a widow in York. The monastery gives money to ten widows from the city every Sunday.

Mary and **Alice** work in the abbey laundry. The monastery also employs lots of people from York as servants in their bakery, brewery and kitchens.

Blind Tom is one of the poor people fed by the monks every day.

Why did the monasteries cause arguments?

The monasteries were under attack for two reasons:

Beliefs: the Protestants criticised them because they said this was yet another example of people trying to win their way to heaven by doing good things. Luther believed that there was nothing special about taking vows to become a monk and cutting yourself off from the world. God was not interested in this. The only way to get to God was through Jesus Christ. Luther wrote a book about monasteries encouraging all monks to leave the monasteries and abandon their vows.

Wealth: others criticised the monasteries for selfish reasons because they wanted to get hold of their money. They invented stories to justify closing down the monasteries and taking their wealth. They said that because the monasteries had got rich the monks had got lazy and immoral. Monks were drinking and entertaining women. They neglected their work and did not really help the poor. They even paid other people to pray their prayers for them. There may have been some monasteries like that but it was not true of all them.

Sir John, a rich local landowner, has given the abbey a large sum of money. This is to pay the monks to pray every day that his dead wife will go quickly to heaven.

There were also many **nunneries**, which were usually smaller but did similar work.

Henry VIII: medieval or modern?

In this section you have been studying how ideas were changing during the Renaissance and the Reformation. To sum it up you are going to look at one person, King Henry VIII, who ruled England at the end of this period. Were his ideas medieval – just like all the other kings you have studied in this book; or was he a modern man?

ACTIVITY

The best way to find out about someone's ideas and attitudes is to study their actions – what they do or don't do.

1 Work in groups and choose one of these topics.
- War
- Power
- Religion
- Caring for the people
- Science

2 Choose any cards on this spread that are useful for your topic. NB Some cards may be useful for more than one topic. Some topics have more cards than others.

3 Once you have gathered your evidence decide where Henry belongs on this scale:

Old, medieval ideas   **New, modern ideas**

4 Be ready to explain your reasons for positioning him where you did.

5 Once all the topics have been placed take a class vote: where would you put Henry on the scale?

a

He spent much effort (and a lot of English money) fighting wars against the old enemy France. He did not win!

b

One of his heroes was Henry V – the last English king to win great victories over France.

c

Unlike the King of Spain he did not send any English ships on expeditions to look for new trade routes or new countries.

d

When he first heard about Luther's Protestant ideas Henry wrote a book attacking the new ideas. He was given a title by the Pope: Defender of the Faith.

e

When the Pope would not give him a divorce from Catherine of Aragon he broke away from the Catholic Church, made himself King of England and gave himself a divorce.

f

He closed down all the monasteries – which were one of the most important ways that poor people got help.

g

When he did finally get a son he had him educated by Protestants because he thought they were the cleverest people with the most enquiring minds.

h

He took all the land from the monasteries and kept some of it himself to pay for his wars, but he gave the rest to his nobles to keep them happy and make sure they supported him.

i

When poor people protested against the closing of the monasteries he pretended to listen to them and promised he would do what they wanted but then he rounded up the leaders and had them executed.

j

He believed it was not the King's job to look after the poor. If God sent bad harvests that caused poor people to starve then that must be what God wanted to happen.

k

In 1515 Henry said 'By the laws of God, I am King of England and the Kings of England in times past have never had any superior but God alone.'

l

Henry did not think a woman could rule England. That was why he was so desperate to have a son to be king after him.

m

Henry ordered everyone in the country to be members of his new Church of England and to obey him as Head of the Church. Anyone who did not obey him was a traitor. Between 1534 and 1540, over 300 people were executed for refusing to agree to Henry's religious changes.

o

A report on Henry VIII by the Venetian ambassador, sent back to his country in 1515: 'This King is the handsomest prince I ever set eyes on. He is tall with extremely fine legs, his complexion fair with auburn hair combed short and straight. He plays music and sings well and draws a bow with greater strength than any man in England.'

p

Written by someone who knew Henry well: 'The King, after he had been to church, used to send for Sir Thomas More [his top adviser] and discuss with him new ideas about astronomy, geometry, politics and many other subjects. And sometimes they used to go up to the roof and talk about the movement and positions of the stars and the planets.'

n

In 1515 the Venetian ambassadors wrote a report on Henry who was then in his 20s. 'The King looks like St George on horseback. He jousted for three hours and excelled all others, breaking many lances and unhorsing his opponents.'

q

'If cutting off my head could win him a castle in France, then my head would be sure to go.' Sir Thomas More, Henry's friend and Chancellor who was executed on Henry's orders.

r

Henry had his wife Queen Anne Boleyn executed in 1536 after she did not have the son that Henry wanted.

s

Henry was very keen on the navy and his favourite ship, the Mary Rose, built in the first year of his reign, was the most advanced warship of its time.

THE BIG STORY:
Ideas and Beliefs Part One

ACTIVITY

1 Make your own copy of this table then write each of the inventions, ideas or discoveries from the list below into the correct columns in your table.

Medieval ideas and discoveries which continued after the Renaissance	New ideas and discoveries during the Renaissance	Discoveries that came much later

2 What do you think was the biggest change in ideas during the Renaissance?

1
Telephone and radio for better communications

3
Gunpowder to make more deadly weapons

2
Printing books to spread ideas faster

6
New techniques in painting and sculpture to make art more lifelike

4
Telescopes to help understand how the planets and the sun move round the skies

5
Electricity and gas for heating and lighting

7
The first regular voyages from Europe to America, Africa and India thanks to compasses and better sails and ships

8
New beliefs about religion which criticised the Catholic Church

In this box are four statements about ideas and beliefs around 1500. Your task is to choose two examples or pieces of evidence from this section to illustrate or support each statement. You could then turn your bullet points into full sentences to make paragraphs.

1 During the Renaissance people wanted to make new discoveries and challenge old ideas. They believed there were many new things to learn. For example:

●

●

2 Some people tried to stop new ideas spreading. For example:

●

●

3 New ideas caused arguments – some of them deadly. For example:

●

●

4 Some ideas and beliefs from the medieval period continued into the modern period. For example:

●

●

9
Iron for railways and ships for faster transport

10
Everyone should believe in God or they will go to Hell after they die

11
Kings concentrate on war and defence. It's not the government's job to look after ordinary people

12
Old ideas should be challenged, not accepted just because people have always thought like that

... about evidence: How do we know about the past?

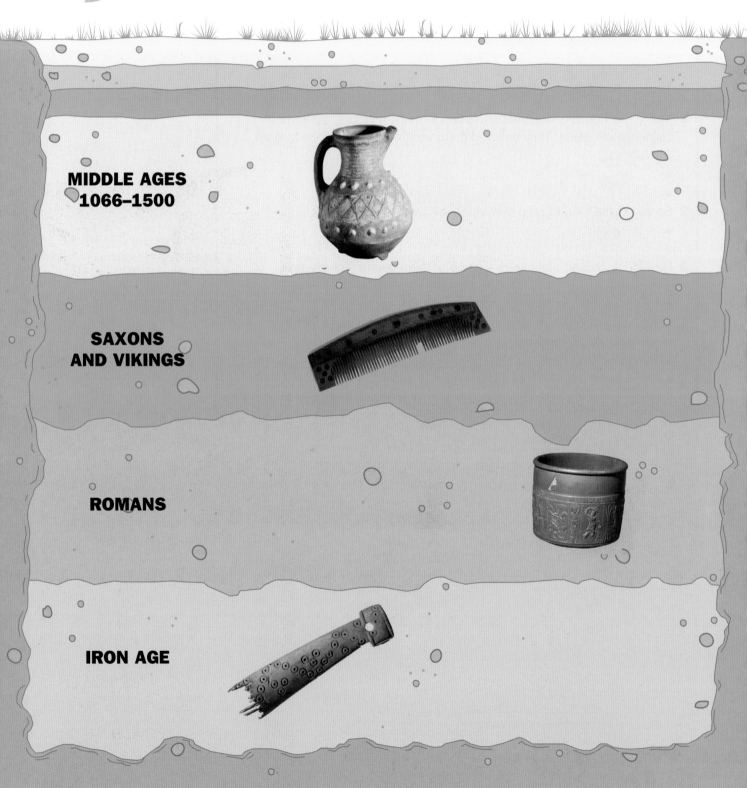

**MIDDLE AGES
1066–1500**

**SAXONS
AND VIKINGS**

ROMANS

IRON AGE

208

Sources give us evidence about the past. Some sources are written documents. Others are pictures. Some are objects. Each period you have studied has different kinds of objects associated with it.

1 Look at the objects A–I below. Which layer (see page opposite) does each object come from?

2 Go treasure hunting through this book. Find two more sources that belong in each layer. You can choose any sources, not just objects.

3 Which sources have you found:

    a) most useful

    b) most interesting?

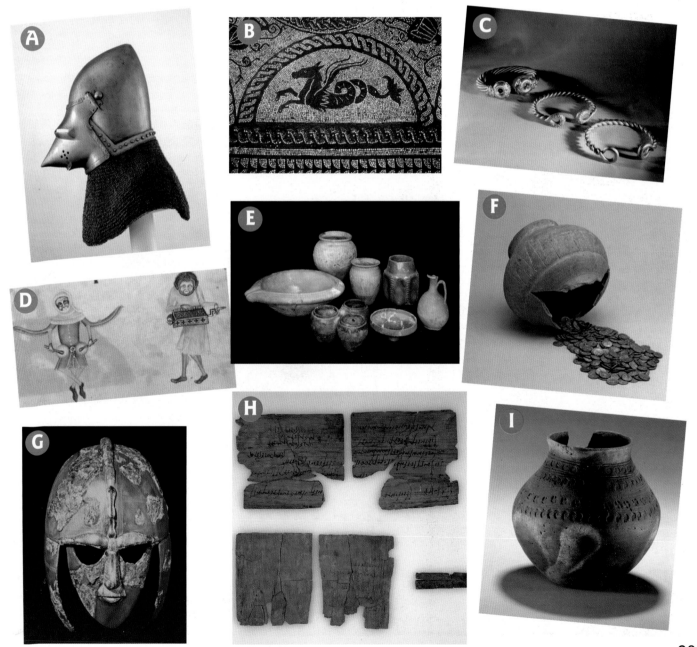

... about periods: Can you tell the Romans from the Middle Ages?

ACTIVITY 1

1 Draw a copy of the table below and put the people, topics and pictures from the box below into the correct column.

The Roman Empire	The Middle Ages

2 Look at your completed table. Look for similarities between the items in the left-hand column and items in the right-hand column. Draw lines to link similar items.

3 What does your list tell you about similarities and differences between the two periods?

William the Conqueror

Hadrian's Wall

Printed books

Motte and bailey castles

Wat Tyler

Slaves

Villeins

Heated bath houses

Magna Carta

Gladiators

Julius Caesar

The Crusades

4 This table contains statements about Roman life.

    a) Decide whether life and ideas in the Middle Ages were similar to or different from Roman times and, on your own copy, write similar or different (or S or D) in the middle column.

    b) If you put different, then fill in column 3.

Roman life	Similar to or different from the Middle Ages	If different, explain what this topic was like in the Middle Ages?
TRAVEL They travelled on foot or horseback on well-made, straight roads		
HEALTH AND MEDICINE · They couldn't stop diseases spreading. · Many people died very young.		
WORKING LIVES · Most people were farmers but there was also lots of trade. · There were lots of rich towns.		
RELIGION They had many gods and were usually tolerant of other people's religions.		
BUILDINGS They were good engineers and built strong stone buildings with heating, sewers and aqueducts to supply water.		
GOVERNMENT The Romans made the whole of Europe into one large Empire with one government.		

Boudicca

Testudo

Saladin

D

211

... about people: Who would you most like to meet at the History party?

ACTIVITY

1 Here are some people you have met in this book, plus a few you have not. Use the index, your memory, or your research skills to work out what the people in each group have in common.

2 Who would you most like to talk to? What would you ask them?

3 Which **three** people do you think were the most significant? Why?

4 Why might different people make different choices answering questions 2 and 3?

A

Wat Tyler

Hereward

King Harold

B

Becket

Edward V

Boudicca

Edward I

C

Robert the Bruce

Owain Glyn Dwr

Alfred the Great

Julius Caesar

William the Conqueror

D

Richard I

Saladin

DOING HISTORY: **Significance**

Significance

Being significant is **NOT** the same as being famous

- If people are **famous** it means that lots of people have heard of them.
- If people are **significant** it means they have done things that affected other people's lives in important ways (for good or bad) – but you may not have heard of them.

Henry V

E

Joan of Arc

Richard II

John

F

Edward II

Edward III

Leonardo

Columbus

G

Caxton

Copernicus

... about significance: What and who is most worth remembering?

1 Three new streets are being built. They are to be named after important historical events. For example:

MAGNA CARTA MEWS

AD 43 AVENUE

EMPIRE'S END PLACE

What do you think your three streets should be called? Choose from the events described on these pages or any others you have studied this year. We are not going to tell you what criteria to use. Make sure you explain what criteria you are using by writing a sentence to support each of your choices:

I think this event should be remembered today because...

2 Now think about just one event. Which single event or person has most interested, surprised or shocked you this year? Explain your choice.

650

The Angles gave England its name and many words we still use today.

900

Alfred the Great and his sons united England into one kingdom for the first time since the Romans.

1215

King John agreed – briefly – to Magna Carta. Later kings also quarrelled with the barons but even when the barons got rid of a king they replaced him with another.

1290s

Edward I started the first regular Parliaments to raise money for his wars. He conquered Wales but could not conquer Scotland.

1400s

The Renaissance spread new ideas about art, science, geography and medicine – some of them borrowed from the Arab world.

1415

The Battle of Agincourt was the latest stage in the Hundred Years War. The English were trying to conquer France. They won at Agincourt, but lost the war.

214

43
The Roman army began the conquest of Britain. Some Britons welcomed the Romans. Others rebelled.

122
HADRIAN'S WALL WAS BUILT TO MARK THE EDGE OF THE ROMAN EMPIRE.

410
The Roman legions left Britain. People gradually stopped using the towns, baths and aqueducts. Angles and Saxons settled and split Britain into many small kingdoms.

1066
THE NORMAN CONQUEST BROUGHT CASTLES, DOMESDAY BOOK, REBELLIONS AND MISERY.

1095
The Crusades began over who controlled Jerusalem. They continued for 400 years.

1170
Thomas Becket was murdered in Canterbury Cathedral.

1348
The Black Death arrived in Britain, killing over 40 per cent of the people.

1381
The peasants gathered at Smithfield to demand their freedom. They failed, but this Peasants' Revolt frightened lords into setting the villeins free.

1450
Gutenberg developed the first printing press in Europe and in 1476 Caxton brought printing to England.

1534
Henry VIII started the Church of England then later closed the monasteries.

Building the History Wall

Asking and answering interesting questions is one way of doing well in History. In the picture below you can see some of the enquiry questions that you have investigated this year. These are the bricks in your History Wall. And you can also see some of the Doing History big ideas that are like the mortar you use to build it.

1 Can you remember which mortar you used with each question?

Next year you will be adding more question bricks to your wall. On the rest of the page are some of the topics and events that you will be investigating. Your task now is to think of some interesting questions about these events.

2 Look at the topics on page 217 opposite.
   a) Use the *Doing History* ideas from below to make a list of as many good History questions as you can about these topics.
   b) Swap your list with another group. Can you identify what kind of questions (evidence, causes, etc.) the other group have asked?

3 Which of the topics are you most looking forward to investigating? Why?

COMING SOON IN
THE BIG STORY OF...

...POWER
Ordinary men
and women
fight for the
right to vote

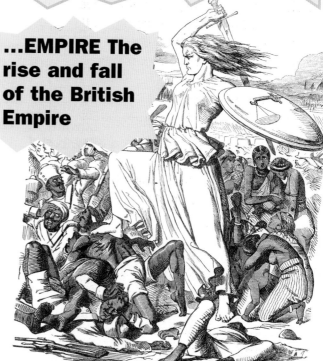

...EMPIRE The
rise and fall
of the British
Empire

...CONFLICT AND
CO-OPERATION
Two World Wars and the
fight against dictators

...ORDINARY
LIFE Civil
rights come
to the USA

Index

Acknowledgements

Cover *t & b* © R. Sheridan/Ancient Art & Architecture Collection; **p.2** The Society of Antiquaries of London (photo: Dorset County Museum); **p.3** The Society of Antiquaries of London (photo: Dorset County Museum); **p.4** The Society of Antiquaries of London (photo: Dorset County Museum); **p.7** © The Trustees of The British Museum; **p.8** © The Trustees of The British Museum; **p.9** *tl* TopFoto/The British Museum/HIP, *tr* TopFoto/PA, *bl & br* © The Vindolanda Trust; **p.20** *tl & tr* Ian Dawson, *bl* © Fotomas/TopFoto, *br* © English Heritage Photo Library; **p.21** *tl* © Bettmann/CORBIS, *tc* Matt Roberts/Rex Features, *tr* Page One Photography, *bl* Brian Rasic/Rex Features, *br* Bob Thomas/Popperfoto/Getty Images; **p.31** Jeff Morgan/Alamy; **p.43** Dreamworks/Universal/The Kobal Collection; **p.44** Ian Dawson; **p.50** © Corpus Christi College, Oxford, UK/The Bridgeman Art Library; **p.52** *t* By permission of the British Library (MS Yates Thompson 12 f.161), *b* By permission of the British Library (MS Royal 16 G. VI f.404v); **p.53** *t* akg-images/The British Library, *b* akg-images; **p.58** *l & br* akg-images/Erich Lessing, *tr* © Michael Holford; **p.59** *tl & bl* © Michael Holford, *r* akg-images/Erich Lessing; **p.60** akg-images/Erich Lessing; **p.61** akg-images/Erich Lessing; **p.62** *all* © Michael Holford; **p.63** *bl* Musee de la Tapisserie, Bayeux, France/The Bridgeman Art Library, *rest* © Michael Holford; **p.73** *l* Malcolm Fife/Photodisc/Getty Images *r* © Michael Holford; **p.80** © Michael Holford; **p.82** © Skyscan Balloon Photography. Source: English Heritage Photo Library; **p.83** *l* © Crown Copyright: Royal Commission on the Ancient and Historical Monuments of Wales: Aerofilms Collection, *r* © NTPL/Andrew Butler; **p.86** *l* National Portrait Gallery, London (NPG 545), *r* Rex Features; **p.88** *l* *Winning His Spurs* by G A Henty, published by JM Dent, *r* Classic Image/Alamy; **p.89** *t* John Warburton-Lee Photography/Alamy, *b* Castello della Manta, Saluzzo, Italy/Alinari/The Bridgeman Art Library; **p.91** By permission of the British Library (MS Add. 28681 f.9); **p.92** courtesy www.paintedchurch.org; **p.96** Glenn Harper/Alamy; **p.97** British Library, London/The Bridgeman Art Library; **p.105** © R. Sheridan/Ancient Art & Architecture Collection; **p.124** © R. Sheridan/Ancient Art & Architecture Collection; **pp.126–7 & p.127** *r* © English Heritage Photo Library. Peter Dunn, English Heritage Graphics Team; **p.134** *t* By permission of the British Library (MS Add. 42130 f.147v), *b* By permission of the British Library (MS Add. 42130 f.161); **p.135** *tl* © Corpus Christi College, Oxford, UK/The Bridgeman Art Library, *bl* By permission of the British Library (MS Add. 42130 f.163), *r* By permission of the British Library (MS Add. 42130 f.176); **p.136** Andrew Palmer/Alamy; **p.137** The Weald and Downland Open Air Museum; **p.138** *l* TopFoto/HIP/The British Library, *r* By permission of the British Library (MS Add. 42130 f.193); **p.139** *t* By permission of the British Library (MS Add. 42130 f.170), *c* By permission of the British Library (MS Add. 42130 f.171v), *b* By permission of the British Library (MS Add. 42130 f.172v); **p.142** By permission of the British Library (MS Royal 14 C. VII f.2); **p.143** *t* By permission of the British Library (MS Add. 42130 f.70v), *c* By permission of the British Library (MS Add. 42130 f.173v), *b* By permission of the British Library (MS Add. 42130 f.158); **p.144** By permission of the British Library (MS Sloane 2435 f.8v); **p.145** © York Archaeological Trust; **p.146** *l* By permission of the British Library (MS Add. 42130 f.61), *r* Bibliothèque Nationale, Paris, France/Archives Charmet/The Bridgeman Art Library; **p.147** © English Heritage Photo Library; **p.149** By permission of the British Library (MS Royal 10 E. IV f.187); **p.151** Simon Webster/Rex Features; **p.152** *tl* akg-images, *tr* Musée Condé, Chantilly, France/Lauros/Giraudon/The Bridgeman Art Library, *b* © Michael Holford; **p.153** *l* Bibliothèque Mazarine, Paris, France/Archives Charmet/The Bridgeman Art Library, *tr* akg-images/Tristan Lafranchis, *br* Bibliothèque Nationale, Paris, France/The Bridgeman Art Library; **p.161** akg-images/The British Library; **p.162** *tl* Werner Forman Archive/Baghdad Museum, Iraq, *tr* Werner Forman Archive/National Archaeological Museum, Granada, Spain, *cl* Werner Forman Archive/Private Collection, *c* Werner Forman Archive/Museum of Islamic Art, Cairo, *cr* Werner Forman Archive/Museum of Archaeology, Madrid, *b* Werner Forman Archive/Topkapi Saray Museum, Istanbul MS Hazine 841; **p.163** *t* Bibliothèque Nationale, Paris, France/The Bridgeman Art Library, *br* akg-images/VISIOARS; **p.164** *t* Bibliothèque Nationale, Paris, France/Archives Charmet/The Bridgeman Art Library, *b* akg-images; **p.165** *t* akg-images, *b* © Stapleton Collection/Corbis; **p.169** *t* Bibliothèque Royale de Belgique, Brussels, Belgium/The Bridgeman Art Library, *b* © R. Sheridan/Ancient Art & Architecture Collection; **p.198** *t* Private Collection/The Bridgeman Art Library, *b* © CORBIS; **p.199** *t* By permission of the British Library (I.B.55095), *b* TopFoto/Fotomas; **p.201** *tl* Bibliothèque de la Faculté de Médecine, Paris, France/Archives Charmet/The Bridgeman Art Library, *tr* Hulton Archive/Getty Images, *bl* Bible Society, London, UK/The Bridgeman Art Library; **pp.202–3** © Ivan Lapper; **p.205** *all* National Portrait Gallery, London; **p.208** *t* © Museum of London/The Bridgeman Art Library, *c* © York Archaeological Trust, *bl* TopFoto/The British Museum, *br* TopFoto/The British Museum; **p.209** *tl* TopFoto, *tc* akg-images/Richard Booth, *tr* Werner Forman Archive/British Museum, London, *cl* By permission of the British Library (MS Add. 42130 f.176), *c* TopFoto/English Heritage/HIP, *cr* © The Trustees of The British Museum, *bl* British Museum, London, UK/The Bridgeman Art Library, *bc* TopFoto/The British Museum/HIP, *br* TopFoto/The British Museum/HIP; **p.210** reproduced by permission of the artist, Graham Turner www.studio88.co.uk, graham@studio88.co.uk; **p.217** *tl* British Library, London/The Bridgeman Art Library, *tr* Punch Library & Archive, *bl* Private Collection/Peter Newark American Pictures/The Bridgeman Art Library, *br* TopFoto/Public Record Office/HIP.

c = centre, *l* = left, *r* = right, *t* = top, *b* = bottom

Every effort has been made to trace all copyright holders, but if any have been inadvertently overlooked the Publishers will be pleased to make the necessary arrangements at the first opportunity.

220